GROWING *through* BROKENNESS

A STRUGGLER'S HANDBOOK

JIM ADKINS

GROWING *through* BROKENNESS

A STRUGGLER'S HANDBOOK

JIM ADKINS

Contents

Acknowledgments

I have often asked my students, while teaching soft skills in our pre-employment class, to tell me a job you can have that doesn't include a "team." This question has been met with some really great attempts to find just such a job, but always falls short when you drill down on the details. Self-employed is never really just self, as you need customers and vendors, even if you are a "one man show."

Believe me when I tell you that writing a book certainly requires teamwork. I learned so much while working at the drug rehab/transitional facility, from a talented group of professionals. They are the unsung heroes on the front line of the drug abuse/mental health issues in central Florida; I will always remember them and their impact into my life as well.

The rough draft editing By Dr John Stanko had to be grueling, plowing through my unconventional writing style. My poor wife who had to hear me rehearsing chapters, acting as a sounding board for my often rambling thoughts. She has been a gentle mentor; I learned to read her eyebrows and knew when or if I was making sense. I love you Lucy.

Then there is my sister Kathy, "The Maestro." If you need some creativity, she's your guy. She graciously poured herself into this project. As with my last book *Monsters and Butterflies: Making Sense of Change*, Kathy produced the cover, did the skillful typesetting, did the final edits and proofreading, not to mention having to answer a thousand questions. I am forever grateful.

To everyone who has helped me hold my life in place. To all who have paid for the truth. My Daughter Lea is one of those who paid for the truths I hold so dear, she is so loved and so special, I owe her so much. This book is dedicated to her.

Foreword

It was the summer of 2007; my wife Carol and I were attending a recovery meeting we had helped establish as part of a larger ministry we share in central Florida. It was at this meeting we were introduced to a guy who stood six and a half feet tall with piercing eyes, hair pulled back, falling down the middle of his shoulders. Dressed in boots and jeans, he looked like someone who walked right out of an Eastwood western and most certainly someone you could not ignore!

During my years of ministry to men and women dealing with addictions, incarceration, or living on the streets, I have met my share of interesting characters. That night there was something different and compelling about the man we sat down with. "Hey BJ, I'm Jim Adkins and this is my wife Lucy," he said, motioning to the pretty, petite lady with a warm smile sitting beside him.

We were taken with Jim's enthusiasm for recovery and the meeting that evening. Jim expressed a desire to be a part of the process. It was a desire that came from a journey that few have been able to survive and few can articulate with such amazing perspective; as I would later come to realize.

Almost three years later I would connect with Jim in another recovery ministry that Carol and I had created for men and women struggling with the challenges of addictions, particularly those who were coming out of incarceration or experiencing a major transition in their lives. Restoration House was a ministry started in 2008 through our organization "Cloud by Day Missions." We asked Jim to become the director of this Christian living facility and to oversee the day-to-day operation.

Jim graciously accepted and over the next few years I would sit with him at what I would call "the table of tears;" the place where we would counsel and help bring direction and purpose into the lives of these young men. I was amazed at Jim's ability to comfort the broken, courageously confront the rebellious spirit, clear up the confusion of distorted perspectives, and pray deliverance for men shackled with bondage; mentally, physically, and spiritually.

He helped these men understand and develop a budget and sought to teach them accountability for their earnings, spending, and giving. He developed relationships throughout Central Florida and connected men with employers, churches, and other opportunities. Jim would go on to work as facility coordinator for a drug rehab/transition center. As such he wrote curriculum and guidelines that were formally adopted and used for training and teaching purposes.

Jim is also the founder of Mark Five Ministry. How fitting! Considering all the accounts found in Mark's Gospel the fifth chapter, from the demon-possessed man who ran among the tombs, to the woman who touched the hem of Jesus' garment, to the 12-year-old girl Jesus resurrected from the dead; it is evident that even in the

most difficult of circumstances, there is hope. The courageous approach Jim has taken to his work and ministry
comes from a first-hand experience that allows him to
identify with those who are in bondage, desperation, or
in the grip of death itself.

It has been my privilege to know and work with Jim,
to witness his passion and conviction, to watch him
speak to captivated audiences of all backgrounds, and
to hear his testimony and challenges. God changed this
"chance" relationship into a friendship of adventure and
learning that has enriched my life and made Jim a close
confidant, a man I am glad to call my friend.

No one I know has a better perspective or understanding of the cost of addiction, the mindset of the criminal
and incarcerated, and the effect it has on the friends and
family of those caught up in this chaos. As you read his
book I pray you will find tools that will give you a clear
perspective, filling your heart with hope, and build a
foundation of faith in your life that brings peace and joy
as it has mine.

Pastor B.J. Oswalt
City Victorious Center
Cloud By Day Missions, Inc.

Introduction

I had done too much and my body was worn out from drugs and drinking, I knew it was too much cocaine, but my addiction only knew two speeds — fast and more. When I turned down that empty street late that night, I thought no one would be around to see me when I used. Imagine the shock when I turned off the inside lights of my car and then realized there was a couple in their late seventies standing only three feet from my window.

I threw all my paraphernalia to the floor while a huge amount of coke raced through my bloodstream. As I started my car, I saw lights coming around the corner behind me. Those folks had called the cops. I flew towards the interstate, and that's when it began — the feeling of pins and needles in my hands, moving quickly up my arms into my chest.

I managed to slide to the shoulder of a deserted stretch of the interstate. It was late thirty and anyone who passed by thought nothing of my vehicle sitting on the side of the road in the dark. My body grew weak and I knew I was shutting down. Staggering from my car, I fell into the grassy culvert, and at that moment I thought,

Is this how it ends? My life will be summarized by a crowd of ten people at a gravesite somewhere and a broken family.

Waking up staring at a blackbird seems like a good ending to this story, but tragically my addiction wasn't done trying to destroy me. Some months later as I sat in a smelly county jail in north Florida having been sentenced to prison for a term of 22 years (a culmination of years of criminal behavior), deep inside I wondered if dying on the side of the road that night might have been a better option.

This is the part of the story where I wish I could tell you about being raised by a single mother in the cold, harsh projects of Chicago. It certainly would help if I could blame my choices on having been dealt such a hand. Unfortunately, I was just a stupid white kid from central Florida. Addiction doesn't care where you're from, who your parents are, or your family's net worth.

Because I grew up in Florida I've argued with my friends from the north about the benefit of "seasons." My friends from Michigan or New York tell me Florida has no seasons, but I disagree. Any real Floridian will tell you we have distinct seasons that range from pleasantly warm to fried hell. In truth, the seasons in Florida can be hard to distinguish. If you told me the weather on October 10 was exactly what It was on April 10, I would not so much as blink an eye.

Life, unlike Florida, has seasons. For some people, they have experienced more of a Florida-style climate. These folks have had ups and downs in life, just not extreme ups and downs, whereas people like me have experienced harsher climate changes of life. I describe my life as someone who has lived multiple lives, as distinct as lying on a beach towel on the white sands of

Florida to being bundled in winter clothing as a blizzard comes off the Great Lakes.

Until I was 13, I lived in a small town in central Florida, known for citrus, a chain of more than 100 lakes, and a unique tourist attraction called Cypress Gardens with a renowned waterski show. For the next five years, we lived on two Caribbean Islands. The first was Grand Cayman, where we lived in a beached houseboat converted into an apartment, and the second was Jamaica, where we lived on a farm serving as a school in the rural mountains of Manchester County. The next 20 years I spent stumbling through life from California to Florida. Those years included a failed stint in the Navy, a failed marriage, and four trips to prison. All those negative events were the direct result of my alcohol and substance abuse.

Let's go back to that smelly county jail in north Florida. I prayed an epic prayer that night as I contemplated what the next twenty years in prison would be like. I said, "God I don't know if You're real or not, but if You are, either take my life or change my life. I don't want to live another day like this."

Now that may not seem like an epic prayer to you, and at the time, I didn't think so either. On the other hand, God was waiting for just such a prayer. I continued, "I can't change. I have a God-sized problem. I don't want to hurt anyone else and my shame's more than I can live with." Notice I made no attempt to make a deal with God, making no promises I couldn't keep. God heard my prayer; He both took my life and changed my life.

I went to prison but this time something was different. Little by little over the next few years, I started to change. What could have been the last chapter of my life became a whole new book. Nine years into that 20-plus year sentence, some guy I don't know won a case in a courtroom I had never heard of. I was told my sentence was reduced and I would be going home in 90 days. I have been on quite a journey since that day.

I have spent the last 20 years of my life back in Central Florida, working in or around the recovery community. I have more than 25 years of sobriety and have remained crime-free since 1989. I volunteer as a chaplain in the Florida Prison System. I managed Restoration House, a transition home for men coming out of prison or drug addiction. Some years ago, I authored a book titled *Monsters and Butterflies: Making Sense of Change*, written specifically for those in a transitional phase of their lives.

I have done these things while working for some great companies. I spent eight years with Brunswick Corporation in their Sea Ray yachts division. I owned my own business for about four years before going to work with Boar's Head Provisions as a manager for one of their distributorships. As I write this book, I work for a large non-profit entity covering three counties in central Florida. In addition to my role as a facility coordinator, I have the privilege of teaching employment skills and criminal thinking, both equal in importance, as I mentor men in this residential drug rehab program. Working in this role since 2016 has been very rewarding.

I tell you all these things because I believe my life experience qualifies me to speak to the issues of addiction and criminality. I have had countless hours of conversations with parents and families of these men who I call strugglers, guiding them to the help they so desperately need. My preparation has included years of working with men in jails, prisons, and transitional programs. I have done classroom instruction, taught practical life skills, and prepared men to take responsibility for their lives in the job market. I have seen families restored and children flourish as a result of men who assumed their roles as present and active fathers. While most of my references throughout this book will use the male pronoun he, I have found that the principles apply equally to women as well. My writing is not sexist, it's simply focused on the fact that I have mostly worked with men.

The problem of drug and alcohol abuse in this country is at epidemic proportions. The response to the dilemma will require the help of everyone affected by its ravages. This book is my effort to provide practical wisdom to both the individual struggling with addiction and those struggling with the effects of loving someone with an addiction issue. In a sense, both the addicted and their loved ones are both strugglers and I will address you as such throughout this work.

This book will not be loaded with clinical terms or concepts because it is not the scope of this writing. Neither will I attempt to lead or advise from my background as an addict with some sort of unique street-wise education that validates my writing. I will simply share the lessons from years of practical experience, shared wisdom, and frontline involvement in this culture. I believe I know it as well as anyone, better than some. The bottom line is that I have paid the price to share what I know with you. I want to play a role by standing between addiction and you — or someone you love.

I will occasionally use terms in this book I know will need additional clarification. I will explain my terms as I go along with the reasons I chose certain terms or descriptions. I will begin with the description of the phrase *addict/criminal*. Most of my students do not reject that descriptor. For many, the two go logically hand in hand and are consistent with their life experience. Others take exception with either or both words based on bias toward the words themselves without any real critical thought about whether or not they are an accurate label for their personal lives. Therefore, I find it important to define both words, *addict* and *criminal*, in the early stages of my class instruction or at the beginning of any life-coach relationship. Please indulge me a moment to do the same as I preface this book.

An addict is a reference to anyone in the throes of addiction. One can be addicted to many things, I make a distinction and apply it to those whose lives have become unmanageable specifically because they are dealing with addictions to alcohol or other substances. Addictions can be and are often transferred and replaced with a new negative coping skill. An addict who stops using a substance may take up gambling or pornography, essentially transferring their focus to a new addiction. The term *addiction* in this book will necessarily involve *life* unmanageability as a characteristic. Let me be even more blunt and direct: If your life or the life of your loved one includes alcohol or substance use that has led to family conflict, loss of jobs, broken relationships, financial despair, or legal issues, then it is *addiction*.

The term criminal has to do with the thinking associated with someone who manifests a criminal personality, as opposed to the act of committing a criminal offense as might be codified in a statute or law. For example, I thought like a criminal which led me to habitually break the law, which as I described earlier, often landed me in jail and eventually led to a 20-year sentence. I was an addict/criminal — I thought like one and then acted out my thoughts. *The Criminal Personality*, a book by Samuel Yochelson and Stanton Samenow, is a comprehensive work defining common tactics, thought processes, and behaviors in the criminal personality. I relied heavily upon the basic premise of that book to develop the curriculum I use to teach criminal thinking.

Consequently, I believe and teach that a person can begin using and practicing the criminal thought process, and many do, before ever having used a substance or experienced any legal issues associated with criminality. At the core of criminal thinking is what I refer to as the "motto" for criminal thinking: "I want what I want when I want it." Selfishness, instant gratification, lack of interest in responsible living, and lying — just to name a few — become the basis from which the addict/criminal operates and to which he or she defaults when making everyday decisions.

The addict/criminal, then, is one who is struggling with an addiction to alcohol, drugs (prescription, or otherwise), the result of which has led to unmanageable behavior. It also includes anyone who uses manipulative tactics to justify or deflect responsibility for their behaviors. I will discuss these behaviors fully throughout the book. Much of what I will be sharing is what I teach my students every week, and it has proven to be eye-opening for many, regardless of their posture or assumptions when they arrive at our facility. You will also notice that I use terms like *troubled struggler* — those in a fight with addiction and criminal thinking and *abused struggler* —

a person close to an addict/criminal who is often being victimized.

My additional goal for the reader is to define *recovery*, which I explain is a process one must enter and not necessarily a destination to be attained. I wholeheartedly believe that troubled strugglers can win their battle over addictions. I do not believe anyone can live sober, clean, and free without first adopting as part of their character the principles of recovery — and then practicing them in their daily lives.

What I hope to accomplish in this book is to identify landmarks on the horizon of our struggle that can launch us, and more importantly keep us, on an upward trajectory leading to freedom. If I am successful, you should have a clearer picture of the process of recovery and how and if you can help. We will redefine some words and terms that will help us develop the kind of conversations that lead to change. Finally, I will provide insight into the thinking process of the addict/criminal, providing a new perspective of what recovery is and isn't. This is important because it will give you a method by which you can gauge your life or the life of your troubled struggler.

General Colin Powell said, *"There are no secrets to success. It is the result of preparation, hard work, and learning from failure."* I will outline in the pages that follow what that work and preparation look like, and offer hope that there are answers. That leads me to the final reason I felt compelled to write this book. Strugglers of the addict/criminal kind are headed for destruction and or death. I am at war with both. I will be going to a funeral this weekend as I write of a 29-year-old whose mom found him dead and alone, lying on the floor. I was spared such horror. I survived and I am flourishing. You as an abused struggler and your troubled struggler can as well.

Jim Adkins
Winter Haven, Florida
March 2020

CHAPTER 1

The Pocket Watch

For the young man thinking about buying a watch, it seemed there was no end to the choices. The watches he was looking at online or on TV looked good, or at least they seemed to look good. Just about the time he thought he might buy one, however, he would read a review of how that watch did not live up to all the hype it was given. Like most he had considered, it was a watch that over-promised and under-delivered.

Many of his friends had already bought some watches but honestly, he had seen some of them fall apart while others never really worked well to start with. *Why*, he thought, *do I see some men wearing such quality watches and they seem so proud of them? Where did they buy theirs?*

At times, the young man had inquired where he could buy such a watch, only to be told he would know when he was grown. He spoke with one man who told him to "just work hard and you will get the watch you always wanted."

The young man responded, "So they give watches out to hard workers?"

"No, dummy" the man replied "don't you know any-thing? Obviously you're not ready. You don't know a thing about responsibility."

The whole watch thing was confusing and frustrating. It was embarrassing to be around men who had such fine watches while he had none. Pretending to have a nice watch was even worse, but it wasn't like guys didn't try. One guy's watch fell apart in the room while a group of men looked on, the glass face shattering on the floor with other pieces flying everywhere. The young man would never forget the look on that other young man's face as he ran from the room.

He thought maybe he would just go ahead and buy one of those watches being sold online. They were cheap enough and after all, he was getting older. By now the young man was feeling like life was moving fast and he was falling behind. Everyone else was getting their watches and the waiting was making him anxious. Then the young man heard there was a guy on the street cor-ner who had some great looking watches called knock-offs. *Maybe I should go check them out?* he thought. "No one will ever know this ain't the real deal," the man on the corner could be heard to say. The young man heard that and thought, "this might be the way to go." At least he would finally be able to sit with the other men and show off his watch. He still wasn't convinced.

He then overheard two men in a diner discussing watches and heard words he didn't understand. After the two older men finished their conversation, one walked away while the other remained, sitting alone at a table. The young man seized the moment and went to talk to the one sitting alone, asking sheepishly, "Excuse me, sir, I couldn't help but overhear you talking about your watch. Sure looks like a nice one. Where can a guy like me buy one?"

The man sitting at the table smiled kindly and said, "Maybe you could sit for a minute and I'll tell you," something the young man was glad to do. *Finally*, he thought, *someone is going to give me the name or a website where a guy can get a good watch.*

The older man began, "I remember asking that same question, not from my father like a kid should. No, my father was the drinking kind, didn't have a lot of answers." The older man went on to talk about how his father had left home one day and never returned. "Imagine my surprise," the older man continued, "when I looked around and saw all these men with such classy watches. A boy shouldn't have to grow up like that."

The older man smiled again. "A quality watch is built, piece by piece. A guy who buys one that someone else built can never be sure of what he's buying." The older man stood and motioned for the young man to follow. "If you want, I'll be glad to give you a few things to help get you started building yours."

The two men walked over to a truck and the older man reached in and grabbed a few books. Handing the books to the young man, he held his grip on the young man's hand and looked him in the eyes: "There is much to know about building a watch. These are the books that taught me how to do it." The old man opened the tailgate of the truck and sat again, "Let me show you something else." He removed his watch, carefully opening the back of the timepiece to reveal tiny parts moving inside.

What the young man was looking at was fascinating. *This watch is neatly put together*, he concluded. The old man cleared his throat and pointed to a larger piece in the center of the watch. "That's the mainspring, it's a power source if you will." The older guy's eyes sparkled when he added, "Remember to keep the mainspring the main thing."

When the older fella had shared a few more things, he got off the tailgate and reached out to shake the young man's hand again. The young man had hardly heard the last words because his mind was already visualizing the watch he was going to build. *Everyone will be jealous when they see it. Dad will wish he had spent more time with me. No one will be laughing at me any longer!*

Shaking the man's hand brought him back from his daydream just in time to hear the older man say, "Work hard, never give up, study the books." The older man handed him a card. "This is my phone number in case you have questions."

Wasn't this my luckiest day, the young man thought as he headed home. The next morning it was time to go to work. Glancing at the books sitting on the counter, he thought, *I'm going to get in those books as soon as I get home. It's time to get busy.* All that day at work he daydreamed about the watch he was going to build. He even took more time on break than he was supposed to because he was on the phone with his girl telling her how cool his watch was going to be — informing her that he had begun working on it. He went on and on about how he had met this guy who was rich and had a cool watch and how the older guy had promised to help him build an even nicer one.

Some of what he said to his girl was not exactly true. It was a mixture of what he dreamed would happen mixed with his desire to impress his girl, all fueled and inspired by the idea that having the new books was somehow going to make his life better. A famous author who just goes by the name of James wrote these words, "Be a doer of the word and not just a hearer, deceiving yourself." There is no greater deception than when we deceive ourselves.

The problem for the young man was that he had only begun to work, had no budget, wasn't saving any money, and had a lot of dreams, but no goals. Goals have a start and end date. They are mapped out, written down, and shared with people who have reached some of their goals so they can point out any blind spots and suggest some strategies for reaching those goals.

This young man had fallen into an age-old trap as described by the author James. The deception he talked about was the idea *that we substitute knowing the truth for doing the truth.* The young man had yet to read a line from the books, had yet to invest in one piece of his watch, but he was dreaming of doing something great, or wearing something special. Nothing had changed but he talked like it had.

Remembering what the older guy had told him, the young man set out each day with the same routine. He would get up and look at the books given him, but there never seemed to be enough time. Before he knew it, he was off to work and then he was tired when he got home. He was, however, learning one important and discouraging fact: A nice watch was going to be expensive.

First, he purchased a case, which was what everyone would be looking at. The young man knew how important that would be and invested a lot into a good one. As the weeks and months passed, the young man began adding parts to his watch even though it was getting more difficult to recall all that the older guy had told him. He did remember to "keep the mainspring the main thing," and at least he still had the books.

To say that after a while the young man was disappointed would be an understatement. *The watch should have been working by now,* he sighed. He had not read the books in their entirety but he went ahead and bought parts, often overpaying, and then placing them in the watch as he thought best. The young man thought, *It looks like all the other watches are working. Why not mine? Must be something in the way I put it together. I suppose there is nothing to do but open it up and try again. Surely, it's a simple fix and we can get this thing ticking. How big a deal can it be?*

In his frustration, the young man adjusted some of the parts, but he read the books less and less, relying on instinct and what he thought was best. He tinkered and repositioned the parts, and bought different versions of the same parts. *Someone told me once,* the young man remembered, though God only knew who had said it, *that people always make these things more complicated than they need to be, like adding parts that don't have anything to do with how the watch works.* He mused, *perhaps listening to other people and doing things the way they did it is messing up my watch. All I need to do is get rid of the extra stuff. It's too much work and isn't necessary. I just need to get on with my life.*

Finally, the second hand on the young man's watch started moving. *I knew I could do it. People think they know everything, always trying to tell other people how to do stuff. We can do whatever we put our mind to!*

Sadly, not too much time passed before the young man realized the hands of his watch were moving — but in the wrong direction. He was angry but consoled himself by thinking, *it doesn't even matter. Nobody ever really gets it perfect!*

He was so impressed that the watch was in motion that he chose to ignore the other details. He resolved in his heart, *if anyone asks if I know what time it is, I'll just tell them to mind their own business. It's my watch anyway. Who says it has to work like everyone else's? Who decided that a watch has to work like this or that? If people start getting into my business, I'll tell them to pay attention to their own watch. "Why are you worried about how mine works?"*

It would have been good to ask the older guy who had built a good watch, *but he would probably look at me like I was weak or stupid.* He looked at the man's card many times but didn't call, justifying not calling by thinking, *my watch is basically right. Just a few little tweaks and my watch will be just fine. Besides it's not like there's a deadline, I've got plenty of time to figure this out.*

He believed if he was given enough time, things would have a way of working themselves out. *What is so wrong with my watch the way it is? Just because it's not like the others doesn't mean it's not working. Not everybody has the same watch and no one can judge me. They're a bunch of haters anyway.* If the young man had been honest, he would have admitted what was becoming increasingly clear: *There is more to watch building than he imagined.*

Building a Life, Not a Watch

I hope you realize by now that the story above is filled with metaphors and is not real story about a watch; it's about you — or someone you know. Countless times I have spoken to those whose lives are in chaos and I've heard some version of that watch story. The difference is that all the pieces that make life tick were not laid out before us. I have heard many stories of difficult life circumstances beyond the control of those I was counseling. We are not always fully responsible for taking apart our lives or for much of the brokenness with which we must deal in ourselves and others.

Still, as we matured, we began the work of putting together something complex and fragile just like the young man's watch. We were tasked with taking pieces of this puzzle called life and fitting them together so they all functioned productively and properly, sometimes without a real understanding of what pieces go where or how they all fit and function together.

Poor timing (pardon the pun) and a lack of priorities and values caused us to put our lives together any way we could. We crammed events and attitudes in, slammed the lid, and hoped it would all work out. We got into relationships before we had a job, bought a car before we built credit, or had (or fathered) babies before we opened bank accounts.

The result was and is not unlike the watch story. We ignored the advice of others, made poor choices, and expected it all to work — and got angry when it didn't. Most of the time the result was not the result of planned choices at all but random events. To say, as many do, that "life happens" is a lame excuse for avoiding responsibility for the toxic messes we create.

There is a reason why certain people's lives work so well. It's not luck or fate. It is a process of careful thought, hard work, discipline, and knowing and *following* the directions. Yes, there are directions and a process that increases your chances of success. At first, it always seems easier to do what "feels good" and then blame others when our watches don't tick.

If adding things and people randomly to our lives is not confusing enough, then we ignore (or remove) certain aspects of what has been successfully proven to be basic life principles because they are hard or time consuming. Like the watch, our life can be running but not getting us anywhere — or even going in the wrong direction.

It's not that we have been given bad information which created the malfunction. The young man in our parable "looked at the books" he had been given every day (for a while) but there was no mention of him ever reading the books. He had the older man's number and could have called any time but because of pride he chose not to. Finally, the young man in the parable compromised with the truth he had been given, cutting corners and taking shortcuts. Eventually he decided to freelance rather than follow the instructions or seek help. We often accept the delusion of our addiction or affliction that tells us certain things we have been told are simply getting in the way of our having a life. We say things like, "I don't have time to go to school," or "I can save money after we're married." Never mind that the second hand of our life is "running backward." Like a car racing down the road in the wrong direction, so it is with us — doing a lot but getting further behind every minute.

There comes a point in the process of assembling our lives that someone concerned about our direction may ask, "What are you building?" They recognize we are not running well or keeping the right time. To hide that we are struggling, we raise the defense that "everyone is different," as though that means that there are different truths that work for different people. The truth is we are just too proud to say life is not working and we are not even sure why that is.

Pain, disappointment, disillusionment, and resentment become like cracks in the crystal of our watch. We may have a sharp exterior that makes it seem like our timepiece is working but the internal gears are all wrong. We substitute sex or porn for building substantive relationships with others. We replace getting a good job with learning what it takes to keep a good job. We buy nice things we cannot afford in an attempt to appear we have money because saving money and waiting for what we want are too hard.

From my perspective, which is far different now than when I was 20, asking someone to show me how to put life together seems so logical. However, at 20 years of age it wasn't logical, so I didn't ask. I avoided asking for probably many of the same reasons you do. One of the reasons I didn't ask was that the friends in my circle weren't doing any better than I was, and some were maybe even doing worse. Another reason I didn't ask was I didn't want to appear weak or uncertain of what I was doing.

I alienated many people in my life by telling them to mind their own business, all the while continuing to cram pieces of life together as I saw fit and insisting that I just needed to be left alone. Probably the biggest reason I sidestepped help was that I didn't know what questions to ask. I was frustrated and frightened at how little I knew about life, but God knows I would never have said that out loud. My default emotion was anger.

Paul, the apostle and prolific author of the New Testament, issued this warning: "Fathers don't provoke your children to wrath" (see Colossians 3:21). In that statement is the idea that those responsible for parenting or mentoring younger hearts should not leave those hearts without the necessary answers for how life works (the directions) because it leads to great frustration and anger (wrath).

The easy response was to tell myself the great lie that "there's always tomorrow," so I should just keep moving, waiting for some magical moment when all the right answers would come to me. That turned out to be a costly fantasy. Life is fickle and uncertain, and any control we have is short-lived. I have attended far too many funerals and can say with confidence that tomorrow is not guaranteed. Tomorrow will not make it any easier for you to admit you don't have the answers. Admitting your way is not working and that you don't know what you're doing is tough to do — even when you know it's true.

You won't build a good watch until you are courageous enough to admit you don't have the answers you need — you don't know how to build the watch and you're not even sure you want to know or build. You won't have a wonderful timepiece until you admit you don't even know the questions to ask to direct you toward the answers you so desperately need. Until those things happen, you will continue down the same path that has led to the chaos and disappointment you have already experienced.

The good news is there are answers and hope. There are directions for how to put your life together in such a way that it functions successfully — and the hands move in the right direction and tell the correct time. They are not available only to those with degrees of higher learning or who possess wealth. They are available to those willing to do the work and make substantial investments

in their lives. In short, it is available to you and the ones
you love.

A Few Coins For Your Change Jar:

- What could the young man have done differently with
  the information he got from the older gentleman?

- Can you identify some areas where you have tried
  to force some pieces into your life before it was time,
  that created chaos or confusion?

- Do *you* want to change, or do you just want *things* to
  be different?

CHAPTER 2

How to Talk to a Struggler

If I close my eyes, I can still see my father, all 6 feet 2 inches and 250 pounds of him, walking into a room when he was upset. The first clue was his signature expression as he filled his mouth with air so his cheeks were full, with clenched lips, and head shaking vigorously signifying the "no" motion. "This is the thing I've been after you about," he would begin, "and it's a thing called responsibility." After that, the speech took on specific bullet points directed my way after one of my latest escapades.

Most of what was said after those famous opening lines I heard many times as a boy, included some catchphrases like "grow up, act like a man, you're not a child anymore." The speech ended with "straighten up and fly right," which I think had something to do with World War II. All these things were true but added little value to any real dialogue about where my head was at, and how life could or should be lived out.

As it turned out, my father taught me some solid stuff — he gave me some good watch parts — and a strong work ethic was high on his priority list. Unfortunately, much of what I gained from him has been learned and appreciated in retrospect. He was there every day and was a good provider. Unfortunately, we never had the kind of intimate relationship through which he could have spoken *with* me instead of *at* me. I was blessed to have a father who cared at all, and I realize that the older I get.

I have worked with young men for years now, most of them in the addict/criminal category. The stories I have heard are chilling, often unspeakable, of boys with no fathers or worse, fathers who were or are addicts and criminals — and were and are abusive. This caused these young men to stumble into life damaged, insecure, and confused. They desperately needed someone to tell them how they got to get a good watch.

It is as if a 10,000-piece puzzle has been dumped in their lap with no picture on the front of the box — or they had to construct their watch with no directions. Feeling unprepared and overwhelmed, they looked for an answer, some reference point, when all too often what they received was "bumper sticker psychology." They would hear people say things like "get it together," or "you're in the real world now," neither of which provides tangible, concrete direction. Well-intentioned people, who say such things with a good heart, assume we have a definition for these terms or others like it, when in fact many times nothing could be further from the truth.

I have had the honor over the years to teach these young men specific life skills about manhood and maturity definitions, how to deal with addiction, how to establish and follow values, and recovery/relapse issues. In addition, we worked out budgets, learned job skills, resume preparation, and interviewing. Then there are basic life skills like credit, education and training, time management, and the list goes on. I included resources for all these topics and others, as well as leading conversations that could advance change.

Watching young men take to heart some of these concepts, I can see confidence grow. I want to share some of those conversations in this book. I hope to give the struggling loved ones of the addict/criminal some direction on how to approach these conversations and the topics of discussion that matter.

Direct, redirect, self-direct is the process by which we cultivate change. Like a seed planted, we cannot sit and stare at the dirt, angry when we don't see the results. We cannot keep digging it up and starting over. We plant, water, cultivate and then commit the outcome to God.

Journey to Eureka

I have conducted an exercise in class settings that begins with a "Journey to Eureka." I ask the group to tell me how to get to Eureka. The answers range from "Google it," to something more philosophical. The fact that they don't know what I mean by *eureka* makes it all the more interesting. My reference to eureka involves a geographical location for some but it soon becomes a moment of revelation that they don't really know to what I am referring, and therefore they can't possibly know how to get there. This provides the entre I need to start a discussion with them about their struggle.

How difficult would it be to give someone directions to a location they were not even sure existed? What if it did exist but you yourself were not sure in what state or country it was located? How could you give directions? How do you get or direct someone somewhere without a reference point? Without clear direction, the chances of anyone getting there would be difficult.

When God allows you to "help" someone in the struggle or you are cast into the role not voluntarily but simply because addiction or criminality have captured a loved one or a family member, your first instinct can be to ask, "How can I help?" That is a loaded question, one that should be addressed with careful thought. This is, however, where the addict/criminal will be glad to assist with a ready diagnosis and treatment plan. His or her version of help will likely be something like "give me some money," "bail me out of jail," "buy me another car," or "let me come back home and live."

The fact is that addict/criminals have no idea how to rescue themselves. They are flailing in the deep water of their dysfunction and if you swim up to them without some training, you can easily be pulled under with them. Like any drowning victim, their intention is never to drown their rescuer but tragically it happens far too often.

Parents often feel their parenting skills should suffice in these life events. When they do, they may find themselves frustrated or deeply hurt when they don't see a positive response from the addict/criminal. It can be crushing to be lied to and deceived, realizing your loved one is an addict/criminal. When this lifestyle is practiced for some length of time, it is possible for the struggler to lose all semblance of a conscience. Therefore, loved ones, family members, and those trying to help the addict/criminal will find themselves repeatedly saying, "I can't believe they did that."

The prisons in this country are filled with men whose consciences were dulled by drug and alcohol abuse or completely lost when trauma and abuse became normative. I have, however, watched as strugglers begin the process of recovery in direct response to experienced people acting as a conscience of sorts for the addict/criminal, recounting for the struggler the painful events of their lives as strugglers.

Serita Jakes, wife of Bishop T.D. Jakes, is credited with a profound remark to her husband regarding a certain lady's embarrassing attire when she said, "Isn't it sad that she doesn't have a friend or a mirror." That remark can be applied as well to your addict/criminal loved one. Addiction causes blindness, at least in some areas of the addict/criminal's life. *It is therefore necessary that someone in a position of influence in the life of these strugglers becomes a "mirror."* It is vital that the addict/criminal revisit certain events and view them from the victim's perspective. However, confronting the addict/criminal in this manner can be a daunting task.

For many, we find the act of confrontation difficult, if not impossible, and that is understandable. In the community of strugglers, some are not only comfortable with taking this approach, they also recognize that for them this is therapy. Some former addict/criminals have a unique perspective enabling them to mirror clearly for the struggler his or her defects. This is one of the immense benefits of a 12-step program. My personal choice is a Celebrate Recovery style program because I believe it to be more transformative, if done in conjunction with counseling/mentoring.

An overseer of a group of churches was speaking to some pastors who were concerned about having invested in the lives of so many people with no results, only to discover that these same people were attending the church of another pastor and doing well. Perhaps there was an underlying belief that they should have been able to reach these people, or that it somehow reflected poorly on them that people started flourishing elsewhere even though they were receiving the same basic instruction at their church.

The overseer wisely gave them an example from agriculture that the Apostle Paul quoted; "one plants, another waters, and God gives the increase." The wisdom here is that none of us has all the answers or resources necessary to help the addict/criminal. Different seasons and different levels require different approaches. Any notion you have that you alone can bring about change will lead to emotional collapse.

For those who have reached the "end" with the addict/criminal and have made the decision that they are done with this troubled struggler, I ask you to consider the possibility that your role at this time is to enlist the help of others. When we find ourselves exasperated, it is more than likely because we have overestimated our influence or capabilities.

For those who have decided that no amount of abuse will deter you from "being there" for your troubled struggler, I beg you to consider the possibility that you are being emotionally blinded to the harm levied against those in your home or near you by this decision. Far too often the addict/criminal gets all the attention, while others in the home are expected to understand because your Jimmy or Suzie has issues. Trying to fill a gap in the life of one struggler while creating a deficit in the life of others is a huge mistake made by families and can have lasting consequences. The number of relationships damaged by a son or daughter in addiction is staggering because emotional involvement often distorts your objectivity. The sad part is that it wasn't or isn't necessary. Let me try and illustrate this with an absurd example.

You and your spouse rent out a spare room to help pay the bills. As careful as you were in vetting your renter, things have gone bad and it's time to make a decision. Your renter is smoking pot in the house, bringing in strangers to stay the night, and comes in at all hours, often drunk. All these things were discussed and prohibited in the agreement. Attempts to talk to this individual have proved confrontational and threatening and to make matters worse, he is not working nor has he paid his rent. Food is missing from the fridge and it is suspected that he may have pawned some of your tools.

Do either of you say, "He really has a good heart, I can't stand the thought of him being hungry, I don't care what you say, honey, I'm not throwing him out." As I said, it's an absurd example. What if I told you this and similar conversations happen daily? As ridiculous as this sounds, I need only change the scenario to say, "You and your spouse have a son in your home, as careful as you were to raise him with some respect and common sense, things have gone bad. ..."

Knowing when to rescue and when to step aside can be heart-wrenching. Having been on both sides of that decision many times, I can honestly say I've gotten it wrong. Shutting the door physically or emotionally to someone we love or care deeply about is as hard a decision as an abused struggler will have to make with a loved one. Making the right decision at the right time is what you wrestle with. Like me, you might at times also get it wrong; we are humans in a fight against an insidious invisible enemy. For decisions made in the "fog of war," there is grace. We do not fight alone who acknowledge God is with us.

If you think you may have lost your objectivity, then it's time to go find some. Winning the battle with your loved one requires that you "fight in the light." Keeping your struggle in the dark is a losing proposition, yet the one many choose first. Some people spend years "protecting" the struggler by covering for their increasing dysfunction. Others spend years trying to protect themselves or the reputation of the family because of an assumed belief that their struggle is unique and others will be shocked or wonder what may have caused such an anomaly. After years of widespread addiction and mental health issues ravaging our families nationwide, the sooner you drag these issues into the light the better. As I am so often heard to say in my classrooms, "You are only as sick as your secrets."

CHAPTER 3

I Say, But They Heard

The Scale

The story is told of a man who every Friday stopped to see his old friend, who was a shop owner, to buy a pound of rice, and did so for years. Come Friday, the old shopkeeper would place the rice in a wrapped package in anticipation of this weekly visit from his old friend.

The old-timers would spend a few minutes talking about their week and checking on the health and well-being of family and friends. The rice, neatly packaged, would change hands and the buyer would make his way home.

On this particular day, after some back and forth between old friends, the package of rice exchanged hands and as usual, the man headed towards his home. This time, however, something was different. The rice package felt lighter in his hands.

He stopped and "weighed" the package, first left hand then right. *No, he thought, this is only a half-pound.* My friend has given me the wrong package. Immediately he returned to his shop owner friend to clear up what was an obvious mistake.

Upon his arrival, he shared his concerns with his friend who was startled to hear such a mistake had been made. Taking the package in his hands he weighed the rice from one hand to the other. After a moment the shop owner smiled and said, "Many years I have been weighing this package for you, the weight is correct. This is one pound."

The buyer smiled back and said "How many years have I come and bought this rice from you? Surely, I know a half-pound when it is in my hand." The moment had now become a little uncomfortable, for over the years these friends had never had a disagreement about weight or the cost of goods.

At last, the shop owner said, "Let's place it on the scale friend and see." The man agreed and they placed the package on the scale, each man grinning as they were certain of their positions, ready to enjoy a laugh at the expense of their friend when the other realized his mistake.

When the scale stopped its teeter and came to rest at the three-quarter pound mark, the men laughed at the result, knowing they were both off the mark.

The lesson in the story is found on the scale. It was a measure that both agreed was true, one that was not based on feeling or opinion.

In the mind of the addict/criminal, the truth is a scarce commodity. Objective truth has been replaced with opinion and feeling. In other instances, concepts have never really been introduced or have taken on definitions that produce confusion when trying to communicate.

It never ceases to amaze me how words like *friend* or *love* can be so difficult to define with any real clarity. Many of the strugglers I speak with, when asked to define *maturity*, do so with great difficulty, if at all. My point is that we must be careful that everyone have an accurate definition of terminology and the objectives we are pursuing when we work with a troubled struggler.

If you have ever had a conversation with someone in the addict/criminal struggle and walked away frustrated because it seemed they were devoid of understanding of the most basic concepts of life, you are not alone. What might be happening is that our words and the associated definition we recognize are being lost in translation as cultures "evolve." I found this to be true in my conversations with the addict/criminal. I started identifying the use of certain terms that were not consistent with the associated definition I understood. Additionally, I found that culture had redefined the parameters to ideas of morality and truth, which become a game with moving goalposts.

My approach to handling this dilemma with the troubled strugglers with whom I work is first to establish common ground by restoring clear definitions to certain words so we can share some mutual determinations about life, particularly why the life of the troubled struggler is not working while mine is. In the end, as long as the addict/criminal can argue philosophy, religion, laws, or even treatment plans, it becomes difficult for them to see that they are sitting in a heap of destruction of their own creation — be it in rehab, an incarcerated setting, or in the wrenching throes of addiction. In contrast, my life is surrounded by hope, loving people, healthy habits, and

30 years without an addiction. I share truths reflected in life experience.

I would like to spend a little time defining some words and terms in the coming chapters. *If you want to have a productive, substantial, perhaps even life-changing conversation with the addict/criminal, it will be important for you both to "speak the same language" and make sure that the rice weighs what both of you expect it to weigh.*

CHAPTER 4
Thinking

"Five percent of the people think; ten percent of the people think they think; and the other eighty-five percent would rather die than think." — Thomas A. Edison

L et's begin with the word *think*. When we say to someone, "you need to think about (whatever it is we want them to think about)," it could be that we assume they will go somewhere quiet with paper and pen and begin to lay out the pros and cons of your concerns about their actions. In all probability that is not possible and even if they did, they would come to conclusions that you find unusual at best and bizarre at worst. Why is this?

If you ask the addict/criminal if they ever think about their actions, they will reply they do. They are not necessarily lying to you but could have a different understanding of the word *think* because they have never learned how, or are not exercising how if they ever learned. Thinking about something requires discipline and technique along with a cogent, rational starting point. Self-reflection, which is really what you are asking them to engage in, is a process developed over time until it is a habit, resulting in the creation of what we would consider a thoughtful person.

You are asking the addict/criminal to evaluate their behavior and learn from their mistakes, to judge what works and does not work based on their life successes and failures, and those in the lives of others. This can be particularly difficult for the troubled struggler due to what I refer to as mind pollution. Bear with me as I explain.

History records a tactic used by those attempting to conquer an ancient people or region. The opposing army began by dumping rocks, debris, or some toxic component into the water wells of those they wished to defeat. It was only a matter of time before the inhabitants of that city or region were at the mercy of their enemy because their wells were polluted. When the writer of Proverbs instructed readers to "guard your heart, for out of it flow the wellsprings of life," he was warning against just such a tactic.

My point is that what we expose our brains to has the same effect. Random, unfiltered, harmful stimuli is like debris in our minds and it poisons our thought wells. A cluttered mind and skewed thinking impact behaviors. Again, if you ask an addict/criminal, "What were you thinking when you did that?" they may respond, "I don't know," or produce some reasoning that is perfectly logical to them but not to you. Your addict/criminal needs to learn how to think once their mind is free of the debris caused in part by drugs, peer pressure, and anger. You need to help them clean out their mind pollution.

How did I go from a wretched addict, lying on the side of the road clutching my chest as life was draining away to someone managing a six-million-dollar-a-year business? The short answer is that God had mercy and spared my life, and he used prison to do that. The process he introduced me to changed what my mind was exposed to. I began to practice thinking and self-reflection. I embraced and cultivated the change that began and created new habits which in turn defined me. Now I can lead others to a good place because I am in a good place.

Hardly a week goes by that I don't sit and listen to someone teach on a subject of interest, taking notes to go over during my "thinking time." Journaling is also helpful for tracking progress and revisiting important thoughts that arise as a result of disciplined thinking. The life of your troubled struggler will begin to change dramatically if first they are setting aside time to actually think and second, to know about what it is they should be thinking. This again is a reason why you may not be able to "reach or teach" your loved one. They need someone to teach them what you assume is a common practice for all.

When I lay out the argument for what real thinking looks like, I ask the addict/criminal how much time they spend just "purposefully thinking" about their life? the answer is usually "not much." I had to learn how to think and your addict/criminal will need to learn how to think before they can address their own life and situation and grow in self-awareness. Once this occurs, only then can we examine some of the words and ideas worth thinking about.

A Few Coins For Your Change Jar:

• How much time do you actually spend *thinking* about your life?

• Can you make a list of seven issues in your life you need to *think* about?

• Can you commit to 15 minutes daily to *think* about one of these issues?

CHAPTER 5

Values

*"A highly developed values system is like a compass.
It serves as a guide to point you in the right
direction when you are lost."* — *Unknown*

The Medina, Washington home of Bill Gates, a 66,000 square-foot mansion, is noted for its design and the technology it incorporates. In 2009, its property taxes were reported to be $1.063 million on a total assessed value of US $147.5 million (retrieved from https://en.wikipedia.org/wiki/Bill_Gates's_house).

I ask my class what they think they would find in the house. Class members tell me what they think they would see as they walk in the front door. I go on to describe a fantasy scenario where we walk into a room filled with paintings, sculptures, and artifacts, all things we have no idea of their cost. While we are on our fantasy tour, I ask them to see one of the guys in our tour lighting up a cigarette, leaning against a large painting, and using an ornate ashtray he found on an end table.

Suddenly the lights come up and the soft elevator music stops playing in the background. A door opens and to our surprise, it's Bill Gates himself, and he's angry! Bill looks over at our tank-top-wearing, smoking miscreant and says, "Hey Skippy, I paid $4.5 million for that painting you're leaning on!"

The tongue lashing continues: "That ashtray you're using is a dish from the Ming dynasty, it's priceless!" At this point, several armed security guards, dressed in black, arrive and remove Skippy from the premises and he is never seen again (which will be very difficult to explain to his parents when we get back from this field trip).

The lesson for my class: Bill has things in his home he considers valuable but for which we have no idea of their worth. Who decided the painting was worth $4.5 million? Can any of us paint something and place it on the market for millions? How does an auction house determine the value? The answer is by what someone is willing to pay for it. Therefore, value is determined not by what we say, but by what we are willing to pay. In other words, it is not what we can articulate but rather what we demonstrate. Words are cheap but actions are worth much more.

When I ask members of my classes to describe their life values, words start flying around the room like honesty, loyalty, love, family, and perseverance, just to name a few. There is no shortage of words and usually, they are all words worthy of value. After that initial response, then I take them to see Bill Gates, the story I included above. What I am trying to get across in class is that a better indicator of what one values is seen in what one invests time and effort. *On what do you invest your time, money, and energy? These are your true values.*

When I speak to strugglers about their lives, I ask them what is important to them, what is worth having or preserving. Regardless of what answers they might offer, my next question for them is, can they show me examples of where and when they are investing in those things.

"Your kids are a value you say. Your kids haven't seen you sober in years. The drunken rants, the fights, not coming home, or not paying the bills is what they see and know." Referring back to the tour through Bill Gates' home, does his behavior represent the owner of the painting or is it more like the abusive person who has no concern for the value of the painting, the one who views a priceless artifact as a cheap ashtray?

When something has value, we invest, sacrifice, and pay the price to have and enjoy it. We also give that which we value a prominent place in our life, like the beautifully framed painting in Bill's home. He hung it in a place where all would see and admire its beauty, and no one doubts its significance to Bill. Lastly, we protect its beauty by placing boundaries as to how it can be handled, including increased security.

"You value your job? So why do you show up late, call off three or four times a month, or go to work intoxicated or hungover? Your family? Really? Why are they worried sick about you? How many times have you lied to them about money? When they try to talk to you about your life, you get loud and start acting out. Where is your sacrifice on their behalf? How are you giving them a prominent place? Why do you handle something (or someone) so precious with such disrespect?"

I apologize if the conversation is getting difficult or hard to hear, but we need to go to a discussion on values because that is where the process of change begins. You need to have real conversations about real things. Those are the conversations worth having. A struggler not willing to have these conversations cannot be allowed to hijack conversations with an outburst or emotional rants to accomplish their agenda, which is to get what they want when they want it.

Why doesn't your struggling loved one take your counsel? They attach no or low value to it. There is no investment in it — no hard work of going to meetings, budgeting money, or maintaining daily accountability as investments into their recovery because they don't value making them or the results.

Why doesn't your struggling loved one keep a job, take care of their family, or pay their bills? They place no or low value on it. There is no prominent place in their life for these things. They will swear by the stars in God's heaven that family is "their heart," but their life says "not true," and facts don't care about feelings. Why does your struggling loved one feel it is acceptable to call you at night asking for money, and then curse you like a drunken sailor when you say no? Healthy relationships are of no or low value. The absence of boundaries produces toxic, dangerous environments.

Most of the strugglers I encounter value self-indulgence; they value their addiction. They invest in it heavily, give it a primary place, and will lie to Grandma to defend and protect it! Regardless of whether or not your struggling loved one expresses some form of self-loathing or is arrogant, narcissistic, and the "smartest person" in the room, the truth is that self-indulgence is still high, if not at the top, of their priority/values list.

So far we have been able to accomplish a couple of things, if not for the addict/criminal then for us. One is that little or no *thinking* is going into the life decisions of our struggling addict/criminal. Two, *values* are determined by what we demonstrate, not just by what we articulate. We saw that we can use two questions to determine where our struggler's values are: Where does this person spend the majority of their time, energy, and resources? What does this struggler invest in, give preference to, and protect? Unless they can get help changing their values, their behavior will remain unchanged, and that's bad for them — and for their loved ones.

A Few Coins For Your Change Jar:

- It was very difficult for me to admit I really valued my addiction. How about you?

- What values are demonstrated by your lifestyle?

- Have you ever dared to ask others what values they see demonstrated by your lifestyle?

CHAPTER 6

Love

*"Love serves and sacrifices, love honors
and cherishes, it is actionable."*
1 Corinthians 13 (paraphrased)

The next word on our list that lacks a clear definition for the addict/criminal is love. "I love you" is perhaps the most widely spoken phrase ever, a close race with "what's for dinner?" I chose this word next because it is also an action word that gets lost in a mushy, dysfunctional swamp called the addict/criminal mind.

Love has feeling and emotion attached to it for sure. What makes it confusing is that it can be tied to emotion in such a way that emotion *becomes* the totality of the definition. The problem with that is immeasurable. Addict/criminals can steal from their grandparents and still "feel" love for them. They can pound their spouse and then weep that it was wrong because they "love" that person. They can choose a life of drugs and parties, neglect their babies in grotesque ways, yet loudly proclaim to child protective services their "love" for the child being taken away. Love is not something we feel, however, but rather something we do.

Love serves and sacrifices, love honors and cherishes. When talking to the addict/criminal, they will insist they love family, kids, spouse, or boyfriend/girlfriend. However, when asked to demonstrate how they serve, sacrifice, honor, and cherish the same, you will get empty words, anger, and frustration. What could be more difficult than to admit they serve and cherish an addiction or that all their sacrifice goes to feed and stoke their indulgence?

The hideous deception is that we will substitute feeling emotion for a particular person or persons for the acts of love towards them. It gives solace to the addict/criminal to still have an emotional tie towards those he is victimizing. If love is just feeling, then all the acts of selfishness described above can be done while loving someone.

However, if love is only identifiable by a set of criteria such as service, sacrifice, and honor, then we must conclude that where those facets are absent, *what we feel is real, but not real love.* This is the part of my class where I watch addict/criminals become emotional. The range of emotions is interesting because it will be remorse on the one hand to anger on the other. It is disturbing to realize that we have abused, neglected, and dishonored those who deserved our love.

The upside of establishing a genuine definition for the word love is that it has now moved from the murky waters of feeling into the light of reality. When the struggler suggests he loves his wife, he can easily apply the aforementioned criteria to his behaviors toward her and determine the validity of his claim. Where it is not true, we can and should call it out for what it is — deception.

My wife loves me, of that I am certain. When in the past I have injured myself, she immediately goes into nurse mode with no hesitation. If I talk to her about my weight or health concerns, she will seek to adjust or modify my diet or schedule. If I call and ask her to come and pick me up from wherever I might be, she is on the way in minutes. I do not say these things to point out any specific acts but rather to illustrate a heart of service that exists in her to make my life, or any that she loves, richer at every turn. She has a heart of service. Sacrifice is key to understanding her story that she wants others to have the best, to put others ahead of herself, to encourage even when she needs encouragement. She will lay down her life for others, for me.

My wife respects me, dignifies me, honors me. She holds me in esteem in our home and among those who know us. She will protect my reputation. She is gracious and thankful. She treats our resources with great care. She is a person who understands and practices honor. To cherish means to take pleasure in and or attach importance to. My wife takes pleasure in those she loves, not because of what they bring into her life but because she loves them. My wife loves me, of that I am certain.

When the addict/criminal says, "You know I love you," they are often acknowledging there is a history with you that has produced a deep emotional tie. I don't wish to disparage that feeling or emotion, for it is real and deep but it cannot replace the responsibility of "loving

someone." If I was to declare myself a professional basketball player, anyone could challenge the absurdity of
that claim. Why? Because professional basketball players
exhibit clear and distinct actions that demonstrate their
declaration of being professional to be true. The same is
true for those who say they love someone.

I think it best I use only personal examples as I conclude this section. When I was an addict/criminal, I
indulged my own addiction. I got up early or stayed out
late to ensure my addiction had everything it needed.
My kids went without to feed my addiction. I knew my
mother was worried sick over my condition, yet I chose
to allow that so I could continue my addiction.

I gave my addiction first place over my wife, over my
little children, over reputation, over parents, over paying
bills. I gave preference to self-indulgence. It was obvious
to anyone who knew me that my addiction and criminality got the golden frame. I took pleasure in and attached
importance to getting high. I loved me, and what I felt
for everything and everyone else was dysfunctional,
self-centered feelings.

What's the takeaway? When you hear the words, *I
love you,* or more importantly before you say the words,
be honest about the facts. Given the criteria for love I
have described, if we took you to court and charged you
with love, would you be found guilty?

Can you hear the conversation starting to change?
When your struggler gives you space to speak into their
life, how much different would the conversation be if we
could come to terms with the definitions of important
ideas about what it means to *think*, how do we determine

values, and how do we show our *love,* which is an action word.

A Few Coins For Your Change Jar:

- In light of the criteria above who or what do I love?

- Do I honor and cherish my family?

- What can I start doing to *demonstrate* love for those who I *say* I love?

CHAPTER 7

Friendship

"A true friend is someone who sees the pain in your eyes, while others believe the smile on your face." — *Anonymous*

The next word I would like to tackle is *friendship*. What I find when conversing with some about friendship is how low the bar has been set so almost anyone can clear that threshold. Once again, we have an interpretation issue. Social media has redefined the word *friend* in such a way that it's hard to come to terms with the actual concept.

When asked for characteristics that describe a friend, usually at least three notions are expressed: loyalty, faithfulness, and willingness to "stick by you, no matter what." I don't necessarily see that as incorrect at face value, but one only needs to dig below the surface to see the danger in holding to such a shallow definition.

I sometimes tease my class that I have the same expectations of my dog as they do their friends. What's more, I have greater expectation of finding those characteristics in my dog than most people I called friend in my past life. If I told my dog we will go for a walk and when we return, I will feed her, and then do not, my loyalty would be in question. I have no doubt that tomorrow my dog would be waiting and wagging her tail, her loyalty not dependent on mine.

If my dog saw me playing with and petting a neighbor's dog, my dog may bark in disapproval but would quickly recover or learn to be accepting of such behavior on my part. She would not pack up and leave. Her faithfulness is not dependent on mine. If I am drunk or sober, my dog doesn't seem to care. If I bathe or don't bathe, she's cool either way. If I watch PG or XXX on TV, it is no problem for her — what a friend! (To my male readers with a girlfriend or wife, do not attempt these behaviors and expect similar results. It will not end well.)

Most of what I just said is meant to be humorous. There is no part of that scenario that can transfer to humans and be rational. Crazy as it seems, however, some would argue it should translate and relate just the same. Sadly, many strugglers will contend that if someone in their life walks away from them because of their addict/criminal behavior, "real friends don't walk out." Other such nonsensical remarks or notions might include, "If they were a real friend, I wouldn't have to explain myself," or one of my favorites, "Real friends don't judge."

Real friends would never let you get bitten by a rattlesnake if they saw it coming. Real friends would never allow you to guzzle a mason jar of gasoline. As an addict/criminal, surely you would agree. A real friend would never sell or give you meth. A real friend would never get you drunk in a room full of nude dancers that practice prostitution on the side, and whose handlers watch you, hoping to take all your money either through sex or drugs. Yet you will say, "my *friend* is taking me to the strip club."

"I got high with my friend, I got arrested with my friend." No, whoever these people are, they were not acting in the capacity of a friend; they were letting you drink the gasoline. They were unable or unwilling to have your best interests at heart. More times than not, they are looking for a co-sponsor for their own dysfunction.

Real friends care. Real friends are honest. Real friends will risk your anger to take action to protect you. Real friends push you forward and stand between you and harm. Real friends encourage, warn, rebuke. Real friends maintain boundaries and have expectations. Real friends will walk away when toxicity is harming others. Real friends are a treasure and most of us have precious few.

My experience has been that of guys who choose to hang with others who can comfort them in their dysfunction. Guys want a "crew" that share similar addictions or criminality and the obvious problems associated with those behaviors. Watch a bucket full of crabs sometime, you don't need a lid to keep them. While they seem to all want to get out, what they do is cling and hang on one another, pulling each back down into the bucket.

A Few Coins For Your Change Jar:

- What is your definition of a friend?
- Based on the last chapter, do you have a friend?
- Who in this world would call you a friend based on the last paragraph?

CHAPTER 8

Healthy Relationships

*"Four promises ... I love you, I'll never lie to you,
I'll stick by you till you're grown, and there are
boundaries and you can't cross them." – John Croyle*

The Interview

Good morning. I would like to begin with your relationship with your wife. Would you consider it a healthy relationship?

Sure, I mean we're not married, but I do call her my wife. We've been together off and on for a few years now. Do I think it's a healthy relationship? Yeah, I mean we have our ups and downs, but there is no real bad stuff going on.

So you would call it a healthy relationship? If so, can you give me some examples of how it is healthy?

Yeah, I feel like it's healthy. We love each other. We don't like have any real violence or anything. If we get mad, one of us will just leave for a few hours or if it's really bad, maybe she'll go stay with her friend for a day or something.

45

I couldn't help but notice you said you and she had been together "off and on" for a few years. Can you help me understand that? Why off and on?

> You know how it goes when people go through stuff. I started drinking too much and spending money on weed that was supposed to go towards bills and she started tripping on me. It turned into a thing and I moved out for a while.

Ok, I can see how that might have been a problem. So that was the off part?

> That was part of it. She has four kids from some other relationships, and we have a little girl together. Part of her DCF case, to get the two boys who live with her ex-mother-in-law, says she has to provide a stable home and can't have boyfriends living in the house, so I had to move out for a minute.

So DCF was doing home visits and you couldn't be there. Am I getting that right?

> Yes, at least not during the day. I had to move my stuff out to the garage.

Has money been a source of arguments or have you both worked out a budget that takes off some of the stress?

> We don't have like a literal budget but we do like split the bills. So, like she has housing and food stamps from her DCF case, and they are working with her on that. When I work, I make sure we have a car, gas, and insurance, you know what I mean. I can afford to buy other stuff like if we want to take the kids to a movie. Also, you really can't buy cigarettes with food stamps, I mean you can, but you're not supposed to. Plus, we limit ourselves to

a quarter ounce of weed every two weeks because both of us are in recovery and we don't want to get strung out again. (Stop the tape)

The interview above is not an actual account but sadly it could be. To be honest, some I have experienced are far more dysfunctional than what I just described. The question, *do you feel the relationship is healthy?* was met with a yes. Healthy for this couple meant first we love each other, which we discussed previously. Can we apply the criteria for love? Service, sacrifice, honor, and cherish? Does this couple exhibit love for each other and the children or do they just have a feeling of love? It's probably a hybrid muddy mix of both.

Second, for this couple, who I suspect has a history of family trauma, multiple sex partners, and all the baggage associated with that, their version of healthy is essentially the absence of violence and hard drugs. They have found in each other someone whose dysfunction matches their own. Furthermore, this couple lacks coping skills, has not learned to disagree without drama, and are involved in welfare fraud (a criminal offense) that they have normalized in their minds. There is drug and alcohol use, with a history of excess that has been a problem. Last, there is no commitment to each other long term which leads to insecurity and uncertainty. Thus, they have no long-term goals or any real viable plan to take this relationship into the future.

This is why we take the time to redefine together what some of these terms mean so people can have a conversation with someone else that connects through the use and understanding of common terms. To tell the struggling addict/criminal he needs to develop some healthy relationships without understanding what that looks like to them could prove disastrous. A healthy relationship promotes health and well-being. It is healthy in that it battles dis-ease. Healthy relationships have the best interests of the other in mind. Too often for the addict/criminal, relationships are transactional. They think, *What can I get out of the deal?*

Healthy relationships seek what is best for everyone involved. Healthy relationships can disagree over the issues without it affecting how they treat those with whom they disagree. Healthy relationships have boundaries and expectations; they don't just "happen." Healthy relationships are neither coerced nor manipulated. I can laugh with you but not at you. There may be tears, but it should not be because I caused them. They neither suggest irresponsible living nor should they validate unhealthy behavior.

Healthy relationships naturally flourish, unhealthy relationships naturally disintegrate. Healthy relationships celebrate success, unhealthy relationships are jealous and spiteful. The fact that anyone has been with someone for "years" does not mean it is healthy. The fact that the other person "understands" you does not make it healthy.

You don't necessarily have to get out of a relationship because it's unhealthy, but you must change the way you treat and adjust what you expect from that relationship. Specifically, you must define what you will allow (boundaries) in that relationship. All relationships have problems, the relationships that last do so because they have learned how to argue and disagree. There are things worth fighting for. Much of what strugglers fight over has to do with their insecurity and jealousy. We enter into relationships looking to find a way to heal our wounds of rejection and abandonment. As a result, we sometimes choose dysfunction over loneliness.

A Few Coins For Your Change Jar:

- Can you honestly demonstrate you are in a healthy relationship?

- Would you choose dysfunction over loneliness?

- Maybe we could list some of the unhealthy habits we bring into a relationship, and consider how to exchange them for healthier habits.

CHAPTER 9
A Matter of Perspective

"It is the obvious which is so difficult to see most of the time. People say, 'It's as plain as the nose on your face.' But how much of the nose on your face can you see, unless someone holds a mirror up to you?" — Isaac Asimov

How many men have died over perspective? How many battles have been fought because of it? You probably don't think about the word perspective in those terms. Most people would probably define perspective as something like *how one views a certain thing or issue.* That is a good definition, but allow me to unpack that a little more for the sake of the struggler.

Perspective has many synonyms based on how you use the word. To bring our conversation into the realm of the struggling addict/criminal, I would like to use a few synonyms like outlook, viewpoint, lookout, or vista. You probably don't envision men lying in the dirt gasping their last few breaths when someone says, "It's a matter of perspective" but consider the following.

Soldiers lying in the thick grass of a field hear the rumble of approaching vehicles. One soldier raises his head just above the grasses and sees a cloud of dust approaching from the east. Based on the sound, it appears there might be heavy armor or tanks. Messages between the troops try to assess the danger and develop a strategy for how they will defend their position.

The officer in charge takes all the information coming to him and makes a brilliant decision based on this intel. He sends a group up the hill to get a better perspective. From that vantage point, these troops report back exactly what is coming, how many are expected, the type of vehicles, their direction, estimated arrival time, and several more vantage points from which they can advance to give them a high rate of success in their quest to defeat this coming challenge.

Now we begin to see how my initial questions about battles and dying become relevant where perspective is concerned. Battles, by and large, are won by those who have the high ground, that provide a good "point of view." *Having the right and best view of the battlefield can determine the outcome.*

Perspective is not opinion. Perspective is not a gut feeling or emotion. The wise decision of the ground commander that day was to utilize the men around him to gain maximum perspective. He could have been proud and decided to act based solely on *his* knowledge or ability. He could have been concerned what others would think of his leadership when he asked for others to help him make a decision. This officer could have taken the information he first received and acted impulsively rather than take an approach that sought answers where he was not confident of his own perspective.

As strugglers, we have challenges coming at us, in many cases on multiple fronts. If ever anyone needed perspective, we do. Yet for many of us, we lay in the weeds making decisions that either waste our resources or get us wounded and killed. Our decisions put others in harm's way. We take unnecessary and deadly risks and expect others to follow us into these battles we are certain to lose. Why? We lack perspective. Are you fighting this battle alone, ignoring those around you who could help you reach a place with a better perspective that will lead to a superior strategy?

In my first book, *Monsters and Butterflies*, I wrote about the transformation of a caterpillar into a butterfly. The book isn't about entomology, but rather about the process of change that is transformative, wherein we become "new creatures" as talked about by the Apostle Paul.

Imagine the difference of perspective for the caterpillar who has slowly inched his way across the ground and through the brush. His viewpoint is one of only a few square yards in its existence, its diet has been essentially one thing, and it has lived as prey for many other creatures due to its inability to flee with any quickness.

The transformation to a butterfly provided a perspective that changed this creature's life forever. As his wings dried and he felt his body being lifted into the sky, the view must have been breathtaking. No longer earthbound, he soared; his diet was no longer leaves but flower nectar.

The world does not change but perspective changes the way we see the world and how we move and operate in it. Where do you get your perspective? Who are you calling on in the battle? How reliable is the information you are getting from your team? Funny how a word you may hardly use can become so relevant. I implore you regardless of where you are in your story or journey as a struggler to seek perspective from those on higher ground.

A Few Coins For Your Change Jar:

- Who do you know on "higher ground" that you can ask for some perspective?

- When in life you recognize you might be in the weeds, are you too proud to admit you don't have the best perspective?

- Has the "enemy" caught you off guard because you didn't see him coming?

I hope that you are able to begin having conversations that prove to be more substantive with your troubled struggler. The previous chapters were meant to do just that. The next few chapters will bring clarity to the ideas of maturity. Hopefully we will learn to speak with grace what it means when we ask "when are you going to grow up?"

CHAPTER 10

Maturity

"Sometimes when we read the words of those who have been more than conquerors, we feel almost despondent. I feel that I shall never be like that. But they won through step by step, by little bits of wills, little denials of self, little inward victories, by faithfulness in very little things. They became what they are. No one sees these little hidden steps. They only see the accomplishment, but even so, those small steps were taken. There is no sudden triumph, no maturity. That is the work of the moment."
—Amy Carmichael

G*row up!* Everyone has said it to you, but you know the road to maturity is a tough one and you are not sure how to do what they say — or even if you want to do so. As we discussed in an earlier chapter, getting someplace without directions can be daunting and frustrating. Taking a few minutes to talk about what maturity looks like and how you can assess your life in the light of that model will be helpful at this point.

Growing up is not a one-and-done moment. I am constantly evaluating my life day by day. I can be mature in one area while lacking in others. I can handle one situation maturely and then struggle when challenged on a different front. What I want to do is present some "land-marks" that will help us stay on the road, pointing us in the right direction. At any time, we can superimpose our lives on the model and make adjustments accordingly to help us navigate our way toward maturity and whole-ness. Let's start with some sayings that will give us some direction as we get started on this important topic.

Riddle Me This

Here are some statements, sometimes referred to as riddles or proverbs, found in the Bible. Let's look at them in light of our maturity discussion. Two of these state-ments were written by a father to his sons to help them navigate their way towards manhood and leadership:

"Buy the truth and do not sell it." (Proverbs 23:23).

"Be a doer of the truth and not just a hearer, deceiving yourself." (James 1:22).

"Remove not the ancient landmarks of your fathers." (Proverbs 22:28).

Before you move on, think about these statements and see if you can find meaning in them that is relevant to our discussion.

Buy the Truth and Do Not Sell It

Truth has a price, but what is it? What price have you paid for the truth you own? What have others had to pay for you to find some truth? This writer wanted his sons to know that truth must be purchased, but not necessar-ily with money — but maybe at times it will! The cost for me as an addict was immense. My family paid; my kids paid. I made my mother pay, along with employers and innocent people who never even knew my name. *Truth has a price tag, and somebody has to pay the bill.* The question is not how much truth costs, but rather, do you realize how much you have paid and how much others have paid already for you to have it.

The second part of this riddle is equally important. Given the reality that you have paid for your truth spending time in prison, abandoning your kids, causing your mom to worry, divorce, or job loss, what would you give or sell it for again? Partying, hookers, dope, fast money? Will you take your truth into "life's pawn shop" and get pennies on the dollar? You will if you're just a boy who shaves because real men don't do that. Maturity causes you to care about life and others.

Be a Doer of the Truth and Not Just a Hearer, Deceiving Yourself

Most of us get the first part of this statement, and would perhaps say it a little differently: "You got to put some action into the words." It is perhaps the second part that gives us pause because we aren't exactly sure how we are deceiving ourselves. Let me use the example I give my classes when helping them see the danger of this second part of the riddle.

When you look on a package of cigarettes, you see a warning label. We all know what it says and what it means. It is the reason you may say to yourself, *I need to quit,* and start planning how you can do that. You may determine you are going to cut back, set a date when that will happen, and decide at what rate you will reduce your use of tobacco. Your plan intact, you start to replace smoking with gum or breath mints. You go to bed that night with a renewed sense of peace because the new plan is in place. Has anything changed? No, it may never change, as is the case for many other plans to diet, exercise, or go back to school.

Why the failure? *It happened because you were content to know the truth (you need to stop smoking) instead of doing the truth (actually stopping).* There is no greater deception than to feel good about the idea of change but never changing — to have knowledge that never becomes applicable in your life. You are content for years to nod your head in agreement that change needs to come, but never follow through. Maturity decides and follows through with action.

Remove Not the Ancient Landmarks of Your Fathers

This saying may prove to be the hardest of the three to see how it applies to our conversation of maturity. Specifically, how does it relate to the struggler and the larger conversation? Let me explain what it means that it's all about landmarks. Most of us in the western world think of places like Mount Rushmore or the Grand Canyon or maybe the Jefferson Memorial when we think about landmarks. The use of the word *landmark* in this saying, however, has more to do with actual markers, be it walls, fences, or property lines, which were used to establish clear borders from one property to the next.

One was considered to be under a curse and a criminal, if in the middle of the night a man were to move the boundary markers in such a way that it appeared his land increased by a few acres and then he began farming on that land. Even if the adjoining owner didn't realize it, his neighbor was still guilty of trespassing and theft.

My point is there are boundaries in place concerning maturity. They were established from creation itself, modeled throughout the ages, and are non-negotiable. The fact that you don't agree with them doesn't give you the freedom to "move" them. Of course, you can certainly try, and many strugglers have done so only to bring a "curse" on their life. The fact that you live in opposition to those borders meant to protect you and others does not erase the fact that you are "trespassing," and your life will reflect this error in thinking.

What are those landmarks? Let's take a look at four that are non-negotiable if you are going to claim maturity. I will speak of these four points much as I would when I am speaking to the guys I have been blessed to walk with through the years. Their application is universal and transcends gender, age, or race. While some may argue that my list is not comprehensive, I chose these four "fence lines" as borders not around your property but around your life. They can act as landmarks to keep you within the confines of maturity. Operating within these boundaries will cause your life and those who are under your care to thrive. It is part of the conversation that matters most when I talk to strugglers.

The four "fence lines' of maturity are *living selflessly, living on purpose, living your own story,* and *living with courage.*

CHAPTER 11
Living Selflessly

"But to mean it when I say that I want my life to count for His glory is to drive a stake through the heart of self — a painful and determined dying to me that must be a part of every day I live."
— Louie Giglio

Nothing better demonstrates maturity than our first fence line, living selflessly. Unfortunately, the motto of the addict/criminal is "I want what I want when I want it," which when we peel away the layers of self-deception, we learn that selfishness is their core motivation.

The problem for the addict/criminal is that they become so self-absorbed that they lose the awareness of the depth of this selfishness. If you have found yourself in a struggle with the addict/criminal behavior, you have been astounded and heartbroken by the level of selfishness you have witnessed.

I cringe when I hear politicians or activists refer to drug use or abuse as a victimless crime. Nothing could be further from the truth and it is no more accurate than someone claiming they can throw a stone into the calm waters of a pond without causing ripples. The addict/ criminal cannot deny their choices have a ripple effect on the lives of many.

Babies are perhaps the most selfish humans on earth. They scream and cry to get what they want. They don't care if you are sick, broke, or exhausted. They want what they want and they want it now. It doesn't matter if you lost your job or have other kids dependent on you, they want to be held or fed or else they scream uncontrollably.

Naturally, no one considers that to be selfish. After all, what does a baby know? It is new to this world and has no coping skills. At two or three years of age, this behavior needs to be coming to an end as they learn to ask, wait, learn not to throw tantrums, and learn how and when to use words like please and thank you.

At the age of 16, screaming and yelling, slamming doors, using hateful words, or threatening are not acceptable. If we "give in" at those moments in an effort to restore peace, we are keeping our children from achieving maturity.

The addict/criminal has discovered that he can manipulate situations through fear or guilt. I learned that if I didn't want my ex-wife to question me about my behavior, where the money went, or why the bills weren't paid, I could just raise my voice and slam my hand on the table, walk out, and not come back for a few hours. I encouraged drug and alcohol abuse and made her a co-sponsor of my addiction. It made it easier to convince her to use money that should have been used for our family on my addiction.

I moved across the nation to hide my reckless lifestyle, convincing myself it was an "honorable" thing to do so my family wouldn't be exposed to my way of life. Never once did I lay awake at night, like my mother or sisters did, wondering if I was alive.

I could always point to gifts I had "bought" for my kids as proof I was a decent father, convinced that smoking cocaine in another room or sleeping in the driveway drunk went somehow unnoticed by their young minds. I was shamelessly selfish, a boy claiming manhood!

Maturity accepts that every decision one makes affects someone else. It seeks what's best for family and others. Maturity will always take less in order to provide more. Decisions are considered in light of the impact they will have on others.

Sadly, I meet men who are well into their forties, fifties, and even their sixties who are still operating with the same tactics of an angry, undisciplined 15-year-old. They can fight, drink, and make babies, all without an ounce of maturity. No one can claim manhood or maturity when the fence line of living selfless does not exist in and around their life.

Immature people cannot save money, cannot or will not keep a job for any length of time, are behind in their bills, in debt, buy what they can't afford, and use a check advance company to "borrow" money so they can play lotto tickets. Immature people have children before they have a job. They use government benefits as a lifestyle. They have five kids from four women. They use, blame, and victimize others.

Maturity cares for other people, stands on its own two feet, cares for what it has, and saves for what it needs. This is a fence line that is not negotiable; it is a must for those who will lay claim to maturity. This is a conversation that must take place with the struggler. It must be modeled, explained, and expected.

A Few Coins For Your Change Jar:

- Are you willing to ask someone who loves you, "where do I range on the selfish to selfless gauge?"

- What one thing can you give up for someone else to gain more?

- Are you willing to ask God to show you your heart?

CHAPTER 12

Living on Purpose

"If I wanted to make a difference. ... Wishing for things to change wouldn't make them change. Hoping for improvements wouldn't bring them. Dreaming wouldn't provide all the answers I needed. Vision wouldn't be enough to bring transformation to me or others. Only by managing my thinking and shifting my thoughts from desire to deeds would I be able to bring about positive change. I needed to go from wanting to doing." — John C Maxwell

Let me begin by describing what be a typical day may be like for the addict/criminal. The day starts when it's not necessarily morning. The struggler stayed up late playing video games and porn surfing on his phone. The promise to get up early Monday and go look for work just got postponed until Tuesday.

Nevertheless, our struggler has agreed to mow the grass considering that he hasn't contributed to the cost of maintaining your home and its bills. He walks over to the gas station with the twenty you gave him to get gas, with the reminder that you need the change to pick up a few things from the store.

While at the store, a young lady walks in and buys some suntan lotion and our struggler strikes up a conversation. He is so charming, makes her laugh, and offers to buy some beer and she offers to take him with her to the beach. Three days later he returns to mom's house hungry and needing a shower. Mom has been worried sick that he was dead or kidnapped. Relieved he isn't, she makes him some food and ensures there is a clean towel in the bathroom. Our struggler thanks her and promises to mow the grass tomorrow.

I use this story in my classrooms and half the room giggles, a few hang their heads with watery eyes because they know I'm reading their mail. For those of you who have not experienced such self-indulgence, what you have probably experienced is at least an aimless, directionless, unambitious struggler.

Maturity has a plan, follows through, pushes forward, and adapts to change. Mature people may not know where they will be working in five years, but they know they are going to be working. Mature people plan their life in terms of months not moments. They can be tempted to want to go to the beach with a pretty girl, but they make decisions based on a plan that has others in mind and pushes them toward their goals.

Maturity still wants what it wants but understands there is a process by which we pursue these things. Immature people are always trying to meet legitimate needs through illegitimate methods.

Anyone you know who has anything you value or admire has achieved or acquired those things with a plan. They had a plan for their money and for their time. They did so by having goals, little ones at first that led them to another stage and a higher level through pushing, moving, and adapting.

Immature people have dreams and wishes, but do not convert them into goals. By contrast, mature people have goals. Goals have a start and end date and are measurable. Mature strugglers can explain their failures but refuse to excuse them. They have plan A, plan B, and are well prepared to have plan X if necessary. Quitting or laying down are not options.

Allowing my parents to pay my way while I sit idly by playing video games, allowing my girlfriend to pay the bills while I go from one job to the next, devising one get-rich scheme after another — these are all the behaviors of a child with muscles, a boy with a beard.

Maturity's second fence line is living on purpose. Go to sleep with a plan, wake up with a plan, and review your plan with others who are succeeding at theirs. Be flexible with your plan, be patient with your plan, but have a plan.

One last piece of counsel regarding how to live on purpose. Plans always include margin. What does that mean? I'm glad you asked. It's saving some of what you have in case you need it. Don't get focused on money when you hear that. It's about money but applies to much more than that.

Let me give you a practical example of margin. I need to be at work at 7:00 a.m. It's a 15-minute drive to the job but I leave 45 minutes early. I'll never forget getting a $140 ticket one day on the way to work. I was late, so I was speeding, and when I got pulled over, people from my job saw me. I ended up working for free that day because I had no margin — no margin for error, no margin for the unexpected, no margin for being spontaneous (like stopping for a cup of coffee).

On that same note about work, I have to wake up at 5:30 a.m. to shower and get ready, not 6:00, because I don't want to rush around like a crazy person getting stressed out, brushing my teeth while I drive. I need to be mindful of margin. I need to get some sleep if I expect to function the next day, so I don't stay up until 2:00 a.m. playing videos — it's all about margin.

I bring home $700.00 a week. I designate 20% to pay my "savings plan" and develop my budget from $560.00 a week (80%). Living on 80% of my take home and saving 20% creates financial margin. I work six days a week and rest one. I could work seven days a week, 16 hours a day for a while, but in the end it will cause physical or mental health issues. Rest creates margin, life is a marathon, not a sprint. Margin saves some in case I need some. Margin makes room for other options, provides safety, relieves pressure, and avoids unnecessary stress.

Margin is instrumental in your plans. The importance of having a plan is a conversation you need to have with your struggling loved ones. The plan needs to take place, it needs to be modeled, and is non-negotiable. We are starting to see the fence lines of maturity form around us. Selflessness and living on purpose are the first two, but let's look at the next one. Living your own story.

A Few Coins For Your Change Jar:

- What is the plan for the next 90 days?
- What is the plan for the next six months?

- May I suggest that you *think* about what you *value,* consider those who have an expectation of your *loving* them. Find a real *friend* who can offer real *perspective* and be willing to *reject selfishness* when it rears its head. When you have done so formulate a plan. That is *living on purpose.*

CHAPTER 13

Living Your Own Story

"Choices may be unbelievably hard but they're never impossible. To say you have no choice is to release yourself from responsibility and that's not how a person with integrity acts." — Patrick Ness, Monsters of Men

Who's Mowing The Grass?

Let's start with another fictitious story. There were three men in a car as it pulled up to the light and stopped on a hot Thursday afternoon in Florida. On the shoulder of the road was a familiar sight — a white van with a trailer loaded with lawn equipment. There were a few men milling around and some started to unload the equipment. One of the men sitting at the light who was watching spoke up and said, "I don't know why they let those guys out to work." *Those guys* he was referring to were dressed in blue, the pants having the familiar white stripe indicating they were state prisoners. The same man continued, "Everybody knows eventually they are going to rape someone or commit a robbery or carjacking, it's just a matter of time."

The driver of that same vehicle said in reply, "You don't know what you're talking about. They don't let the dangerous ones out on that duty. Those guys are all petty thieves and druggies." The driver spoke as if he had some inside knowledge of how the system worked as he explained further, "The murderers and rapists get to sit in the prison in an air-conditioned cell watching HBO all day."

By now, the men were unloading the equipment and starting mowers. It was then that the guy in the back-seat of the car who was listening to this exchange spoke up, "What's the guy's name who is mowing that median with the yellow mower?" The comment was met with disbelief, for who would know the name of some convict on the side of the road? The guy in the backseat asked again, "What about the guy with the weed eater? Do you think he has kids?" Now the two other passengers were getting agitated by the questions from their passenger.

That did not deter the guy in the back: "How do you guys know so much about why these men got to this place in their lives? How do you know that these men haven't changed in their hearts and are deeply sorry for what they did? You accuse them of crimes you know nothing about, judge them based on their outfits and where they are right this minute. Are you both the same guys today as you were in your twenties?" Silence filled the car.

As you read that, you could probably identify with the men in that car. Each of us has judged a situation we saw based on what we thought we knew about the people involved and it took someone exposing our bias to bring us to our senses. The definition of preju-dice is a preconceived opinion not based on reason or experience. Examples would be judging someone based on something as simple as their clothes and the way they look. It is how you feel about someone when you don't even know their name but what you think you know, an opinion or an idea you have based neither in fact nor experience.

The two men in the car were not bad guys. Their thinking was muddled by a common view of prisoners fueled by rumors, but no interaction with men in these facilities. I do not find it particularly offensive. What does concern me more than the attitudes of these men is the ones I hear from those who are on the side of the road (the addict/criminal). And that leads me to the *third fence line of maturity: living your own story.*

Those guys on the side of the road will tell me what is in store for them when they get out. They are sure that because of their past, they will not be able to get very far in life or with people. They assign names to themselves; they assume they know what will happen next, they look at their future through the lens of their present situation. They are harder on themselves than the men in our car scenario ever were.

Looking back as I age shows me that life has thrown me some curves. While these things may help explain me, they don't get to define me. No longer will I allow others to write on the pages of my life without my permission. What happens in the chapters of my life doesn't determine the book. I choose to take responsibility for the outcomes, attitudes, failures, and successes.

Blaming others or events beyond my control does not push me forward but rather, it binds me to the past. I am who God says I am, not my history, not my shame, not my enemies, not social media. I will not give a pen to those who would try to define me. I am responsible, I will work harder, I will expect more, and I will trust God with the outcomes.

Who has been writing on the pages of your life? I listen to the stories of dozens of strugglers and the tales are at times heart-rending. Their father abandoned them, their mother abused them, or they never knew their families at all. Maybe their parents were addicted to drugs and alcohol, there was violence or other horrible things they witnessed. Others did not experience horrific events but they experienced loneliness or rejection. I hear stories of children dying, divorce, betrayal, or mental health struggles.

Life can be chock full of events capable of sending us into an unexpected tailspin. How you came to be an addict/criminal is important. There is value in looking back if it will help you move forward. The problem is that looking back can become a habit. Looking back can become an emotional wheelchair for us to ride through years of our life accepting what crippled us without addressing or resisting its dysfunction. When we think about our life, we see ourselves as victims of the cruelty or apathy from those we thought should have cared and we become like them if we are not careful.

The stories I have heard are real. I would never discount the validity of the impact any of these people or events had on their lives. That being said, allowing these experiences to dominate our future is unacceptable. Don't allow anyone to write your story except you and those who love you and have your best interests at heart.

My point is, that we must take responsibility for what happens next. Maturity requires personal responsibility,.

No more excuses. No more shifting blame. No more prejudging the outcomes of our lives based on our past or current status. What *was* is *not* permission to give up or give in. Maturity sees failure as an opportunity to start over.

A Few Coins For Your Change Jar:

- Who are you? Who told you that?

- What will hold you back from a healthy, happy life?

- I have no doubt many of you reading this have been hurt, legitimately. Abandoned and rejected, lied to and mistreated. Maturity says: no more will I allow others to write in my book. I will not let my past define me and I accept responsibility for what happens next.

CHAPTER 14
Living With Courage

"When we least expect it, life sets us a challenge to test our courage and willingness to change; at such a moment, there is no point in pretending that nothing has happened or in saying that we are not yet ready. The challenge will not wait. Life does not look back." — *Paulo Coelho*

In many instances, the addict/criminal makes many attempts to change. The problem with change is that it's difficult. It's been said that the right thing and the hard thing usually have a lot in common. You can try and sell me on the idea that change is as easy as thinking differently about life, but I'm not buying. Change and maturity take courage.

Let me do a quick review of what we have been talking about; the *four fence lines of maturity. Living selflessly* demands we live with others in mind. Selfishness. on the other hand, takes more than it gives. Which of these adjectives best describes you is determined by courage. Living out your convictions in the most difficult of circumstances.

Living on purpose is developing a plan with goals to make your plan a reality. This is the "ready, set" of the race and "go" is the courage. This is courage to commit, courage to postpone good to pursue great. Then, we talked about *living your own story*, which involves accepting your role in how you got where you are, breaking emotional chains with your past, and accepting responsibility for what happens next. That may seem a daunting step. "Fear is a feeling, courage is what we do," said one writer.

Here let me use a technical word in my less than technical approach to courage and maturity — *synergy*. Let me give you the definition and then make my point. According to the *Oxford Dictionary*, synergy is the interaction or cooperation of two or more organizations, substances, or other agents to produce a combined effect greater than the sum of their separate effects. Tell me that's not a mouthful.

Simple explanation is like this. Hydrogen has value, let's call it 50. Oxygen has value, let's also call it 50. Math was never my strong point but even I know that 50 plus 50 equals 100. However, with the *synergistic effect*, when you combine those two, their value now increases beyond their sum total to let's say 300 (a combined effect greater than the sum of their separate effects).

Courage has a synergistic effect in developing maturity. Combined with choosing selflessness over self-serving, living a life of purpose and with a plan, taking charge of your story and what happens next, the *fourth fence line of courage* provides fuel that propels me into the next right thing and the one after that. The more courageous decisions I make, the more courage is produced. In other words, when I combine courage with purpose, goals, or integrity there is a synergistic effect and I obtain greater benefit than I would ordinarily expect. All four together comprise the fence line of maturity.

It requires great courage to live out your convictions. If I asked a group of guys if they want to take a boat out to go deep sea fishing, it wouldn't require a lot of courage to take them on that journey. However, if as we headed out to sea that same group of guys broke out a deck of cards for some poker and some ice-cold beer, how much courage would it take to get up and walk away, explaining to my old pals that I am headed a different direction.

If I met someone at work and while at lunch, he asked if I wanted to go smoke a joint, it really requires little courage to say no because I don't smoke. What if it's your girlfriend who lights up a joint in your car while out for the evening? That is where courage has to kick in. Those are the moments where our character and maturity will be challenged.

Courage isn't always challenged in such dramatic moments. For example, you go to the hardware store to grab some wire connectors and a lightbulb for a small project. Then you see a giant above-ground pool on sale. You have the $600 saved towards car repairs that you don't need right now so you are tempted to buy the pool. Instead, you push that thought aside, choose to stay on track with your plan, and today say no to yourself. When you live with tomorrow and others in mind, that takes courage!

It's Thursday afternoon and you are on your way home after an exhausting day at work. Your mind is tired and begins to wander. You hear the voice of disappointment mocking how you busted your butt all week just so you can use all your money to pay bills. You remember how much money you used to throw around when you were involved in criminal activity. Suddenly courage kicks in and reminds you the reasons you have to be grateful: people trust you, your wife and kids respect you, your bills are paid, you haven't been arrested or passed out drunk in years, courage to do the next right thing rises up.

As addicts/criminals, we try to make every day a party, needing everything to be exciting and intoxicating as we hang out with our friends or girls and have fun. Life is not an every-day party, for even the most satisfying lives have some mundane moments and routines requiring sober thought. It takes courage to push through those days or weeks so you don't trade deep joy in life for cheap fun. It takes courage to avoid trading relationships and intimacy for sex and shame.

Little boys and girls are selfish with unrealistic expectations, relying on others to do things for them. They don't budget or plan their future. They just play and have fun, allowing everyone else to worry about bills or what happens tomorrow. It requires no courage to be a little boy or girl and live this kind of life. Maturity grows in courageous acts.

A Few Coins For Your Change Jar:

- Do you consider yourself a person of courage? Why or why not?

- Have you ever considered it an act of courage to just get up and do the next right thing again today?

- What about the courage to hold to your values, when someone you are attached to wants to go a different direction?

CHAPTER 15

The Dark Mysteries of Recovery

Ask anyone to describe a car and regardless of their knowledge or enthusiasm for them, you will get pretty much the same answer. It will not vary much beyond body styles, engine size, or make or model. There are distinct features that describe a car: four tires, one steering wheel, a drive train, seating, and windows that go up and down. You will never find someone who cannot differentiate between a car and a boat; even a child can make that distinction.

Ask anyone to describe recovery and depending on their knowledge or enthusiasm of the process, you will get answers as different as heaven and hell. It is as if the recovery process is some enigmatic riddle unique to each individual. Perhaps the idea is propagated through the oft-repeated line in the recovery community, "Everyone's recovery looks different."

I'm not interested in splitting hairs with anyone concerning recovery or any one particular approach to recovery or organization. The recovery community is as diverse as life itself and that is a good thing. My concern is not in what community you choose to engage but rather how you engage the process while in the community.

I will put forth five distinct elements of recovery that not only describe what recovery looks like but also include the indisputable characteristics of the process. Just as distinct as describing a car, the components of recovery are clearly identifiable. Being *humble, grateful, teachable, accountable* and *responsible* make up "the rungs of a recovery ladder" as we climb up towards recovery.

If someone were to pull alongside the dock where I was fishing, the outboard motor grumbling on the back of a v-shaped fiberglass hull and asked, "Can I take you out in the lake in my truck?" I would back away slowly, eyebrow raised, worried about the stability of this person. That's how I feel when I meet strugglers talking to me about recovery when they do not display any awareness of the process. They talk about abstinence and spirituality, they quote from the Big Book but I start backing away slowly, eyebrow raised.

I am joking about this because I have shed many tears over the heartbreaking effects of such deception. I have known strugglers who spend years in "the rooms" and OD anyway, drunks who spend their lifetime "quitting" but constantly return to the misery of a drunk. I've worked with strugglers who go to rehab seven times and never break free. The difference for those who survive and thrive is rooted in how well they embrace the five elements.

I shared these elements with my supervisor and she graciously agreed they were true, but was a little surprised I didn't include honesty as an element. She made a great point. Honesty is like reliability or trustworthiness in that it is developed over time. I teach honesty to the criminal/addict, and we could spend weeks unpacking the idea if I had such a luxury. Becoming open and honest can take a lifetime to achieve fully.

Her point taken, let me discuss honesty as it relates to the five elements of recovery. Imagine, if you will, a lone survivor on a slowly deflating life raft in a stormy sea. Waves rising, supplies all gone, a bad situation about to become tragic. Suddenly a Coast Guard chopper appears through the clouds and mist with floodlight shining on this lone survivor waving and yelling for rescue.

That's all the honesty needed to enter into the recovery process. I am in big trouble; my situation is far graver than I can manage. Please help me. "I admitted," the famous first words of the first step.

The five elements that follow have honesty baked in. My desire is to outline what each of these elements look like in the life of the struggler and to contrast that with what it looks like when those same elements are absent, worse when they are replaced with the elements associated with relapse. This I hope becomes a graph of sorts that one can superimpose onto their life, to gauge more honestly where they are in the process.

For those struggling to walk with someone in need of recovery, hopefully this will help you chart a course and develop a framework designed to bring about substantial change. The question that I ask every student, "do *you* want to change or do you just want *things* to be different" is an important one. Most every struggler wants things to be different, but change is hard and not without pain. Change through the process of recovery takes time and patience, the addict/criminal will resist that. At their core is the immediate relief of their pain.

Is the struggler ready to enter the process? When you attempt to rescue them, shining a light of truth and hope, what is their reaction? The answer can be found in the first element.

CHAPTER 16

Element One: Humility

"Humility is not thinking less of yourself
but thinking of yourself less. – C. S. Lewis

Perhaps the most significant indication that an individual is ready to begin the recovery process is humility. Among its synonyms is the word *brokenness*, a surrender of the idea that we can somehow manage our problem. It is the total opposite of *arrogance*, a trait we as strugglers often exhibit in our addiction and dysfunction.

If you don't believe me, ask the parent or spouse of some young man who just called collect from the county jail. Mind you, this young man is broke, has no job, has been drunk or high for months, and everyone close to him has fled or been abused. Yet he's calling them to scream about his having been arrested for violent behavior. "This is going to ruin my life." he screams, "When are you going to bail me out?"

Let me pause here to point out the two most common tactics used by the addict/criminal for manipulating victims. The first is anger. The addict/criminal will attempt to use intimidation through loud aggressive outbursts and verbal abuse that may include dramatic acts or even violence. This is particularly effective with those whose personalities are gentle and nurturing.

The addict/criminal screams and yells, slams his fist, bellows out a barrage of passive-aggressive threats, and storms outside or in another room slamming the door behind. In the silence that follows, everyone left behind stands accusing themselves and the other participants in the fight of mishandling the situation.

In the ensuing days, relationships between family members and spouses are damaged due to real or perceived failures by one party or the other. The mother says to the father, "You can't talk to him like that or you know it will turn into a fight," the accusation may be charged. Instead of the addict/criminal being the problem, those involved turn on one another and make one another the problem. The stress created by the addict/criminal is quite harmful.

The abused wife dares not say certain words or talk about certain subjects. Trained by the addict /criminal to maintain peace at all costs, a "good day" for the loved one of the addict/criminal is one in which there is no yelling or fights — and the pathetic cycle continues.

The second most common tactic used is *guilt*. Tears begin flowing as the addict/criminal weeps out their version of why they are a victim of *your* abuse, how misunderstood they are. Sitting in silence, they stare at the ground and can only mutter one-word responses to inquiries as to the reason for their woundedness.

When anyone tries to address their behaviors, they isolate themselves for hours, days, or weeks, running away or hanging up. If they can disappear for a few days or weeks they will, knowing their victim will be sick with worry and their mom, spouse, or friend will be more hesitant to confront their behaviors when they return. The addict/criminal is counting on their victim not having the emotional strength to bear another month of anxiety worrying about their loved one.

Humility often arrives for the addict/criminal in painful ways, as if we were in a car accident and thrown through the windshield onto the hard pavement of a new reality. We must sit in the self-awareness that we have wrecked much if not all of what was good or close to us. You will see that reality in the eyes of some who face legal prosecution, others will find themselves alone and isolated from family with all their resources depleted.

For others, reaching a place in their hearts that demonstrates humility may only come after many fights, arguments, and dramatic loss. We lose jobs, families, and reputation, constantly lashing out at everyone and everything around us. It is usually true that once we are forced to look back in the rear-view mirror of our lives, pride is stripped away and humility can begin to work.

Lack of humility is perhaps the single biggest reason that addict/criminals go through multiple incarcerations or rehab programs, only to return to the same behaviors. Recovery is not just abstinence from harmful chemicals or behaviors. The fact that they are in a program or sitting in meetings does not mean they are in recovery any more than sitting in their garage makes them a car.

That's why we need to talk about what real humility looks like (along with real recovery) in the context of working with someone who needs to be in recovery. Again, let us make a clear distinction that everyone's recovery looks a little different. Not everyone needs to be in a residential program, for example, but everyone needing recovery must begin with humility.

The humble struggler *has run out of excuses and arguments*. At that point, they want answers, not a fight. The struggler has realized their decisions up to this point have led them to where they are. The addict/criminal on the other hand is continually interrupting with the word *but*. The addict/criminal will say things like "*but* what you don't understand is ... *but* I am not like you ... *but* just because I do that doesn't mean ... I am not a bad person *but*, I just keep slipping up."

At every turn they argue with your advice or resist your attempts to bring accountability into their lives, be it over money management, health concerns, or boundaries. If much of your energy is spent debating the merits or benefits of such concerns to the addict/criminal, then know this person requires a dose of humility and is not in recovery despite anything they say.

The humble struggler *is not pointing at others for the problems they have created*. They are not saying, "If you and Dad had really cared or listened." Notice how in so few words the script is flipped and someone else is the problem. Blame-shifting is not an attribute of the humble. They realize it is not the boss's fault, not the spouse's fault, not the court's fault. It is not genetics, karma, or fate.

It is far too common when confronting the addict/criminal for the discussion to begin with a certain attitude or behavior, only to morph into a whole new conversation. This is done as he deftly deflects the comments directed at him or her and points to an unrelated or irrelevant situation, arguing the merits of fairness or others' responses to it. How quickly the addict/criminal can place others on the defensive about an unrelated issue.

Learning how to redirect the conversation is always a needed skill when dealing with the addict/criminal. I refuse to argue any longer when speaking to an addict/criminal; it has never proved beneficial. The humble struggler does not become angry at words like *no, wait, or let me think that over.* For the humble struggler, any help is seen as a gift. They no longer feel entitled to make demands or impose their expectations or demand the same. They are no longer prescribing how you can or should help them.

For the addict/criminal, instant gratification is at the core of their operating system. For instance, if you ask them to attend 12-step meetings for 30 days at which time you will consider helping them, they become angry and argue the merits of such an idea. Let this be a red flag! If the addict/criminal in your life is demanding your help and will not take no for an answer, if the addict/criminal is calling you repeatedly and insisting you talk, if that person is making demands, certain they know what is best, end the conversation. Hold your position. This struggler is not ready for help.

The humble struggler *does not romanticize his former life.* No longer are the escapades of his or her past considered "great adventures." They are not starring in some unbelievably funny comedy movie. When we talk to others, we tell the whole story, the sad parts, where wives and mothers cry or children go without because of our selfish addiction. By contrast the addict/criminal brags and highlights all the *fun* they have had. However, when discussing the losses associated with this "fun," like jail, financial despair, loss of a job, or loss of relationships, they minimize those events or they shift the responsibility to others. By contrast, the humble struggler is remorseful over and embarrassed by their behaviors. They find the humor of such prideful addict/criminal acts shallow and shameful.

It is important to note that the addict/criminal has learned over time to mimic emotions and responses to manipulate others. Therefore, at times they will feign humility for the purpose of "softening" the person who is attempting to bring about substantial change. They often learn the language of recovery without a single concept of recovery ever taking root in their life. The reason it becomes difficult to fight against such a tactic is, for many of us, our inability to discern when we are looking at real humility and when we are being gamed.

My grandfather had a saying: "if you bump some-one's bucket, you'll see what they are carrying." What that will look like for you, the abused struggler, is likely a hostile response to words like "no." Ask your strug-gler if you can sit down with them weekly to go over paycheck, expenditures, savings and develop a budget. Apart from the humble heart needed for recovery, you are going to get pushback and outrage.

A Few Coins For Your Change Jar:

- Are you still trying to argue your case with friends and family?

- Are you or the one you are trying to help, still employ-ing tactics of intimidation or guilt?

- Does "I need help" come with attachments or condi-tions?

CHAPTER 17

Element Two: Gratitude

*"Being grateful does not mean that everything
is necessarily good. It just means that you
can accept it as a gift." — Roy T. Bennett*

*"Gratefulness is the moment that entitlement vanishes. As
we lay in the ash heap of our own making and see the light of
God still shines, shines upon the hand of the good Samaritan
reaching out to invest in our healing." — Jim Adkins*

For those of us in recovery, we cannot wait to tell others about the grace we have been given. We now see the hand of Providence that has been at work all along and we are in awe. Grateful may not be the place I find myself in at every turn, for I am human. However, it is the place to which I return daily, reminding my humanity of my spirituality and the predominant role it must have in my life.

Mike Rowe of *Dirty Jobs* fame says in his "Sweat Pledge," "the most annoying sound in the world is whining." I'm mad I didn't say that first! Complaining and cursing about your life is perhaps the "language of hell" itself. No one in recovery curses life for long before they are convicted by their conscience and must immediately return to gratefulness.

Some constantly complain that nothing is quite good enough or how other people are not living up to their expectations. Others are in a recovery program saying they can't wait until it's over, pointing out how ignorant this process is or how stupid the people are. The only time you hear any gratitude is when they say they are thankful their time in the program is almost over or that they are not as stupid as others. These angry, troubled strugglers are not in recovery and are only fooling themselves.

The grateful struggler *does not feel entitled or speak that language.* The most common phrase of the entitled is, "How is that fair?" Personally, I am grateful I was not given fair. Fair for me would have been a long stretch in prison, maybe even worse. Fair for me would have been a daughter who disowned me or a body destroyed by my abuse.

Maybe for you, the consequences would not have been so dire. But I suspect the reason some don't clearly see how life could be drastically different without the people and opportunities that have been given them is in part due to the blindness of being ungrateful.

Don't be fooled by the mountains of platitudes or the buckets of tears, for the addict/criminal has plenty to spare. Not to say that tears or expressions of gratitude aren't real, but the true test is in what they *demonstrate* not just what they *articulate.* Being grateful is a lifestyle.

One difference between a contract and a bill is that one requires a signature while the other requires an investment. Gratitude is a daily investment in my environment.

I must show that I am grateful. When my words are not reflected in my life, I raise another red flag!

The grateful struggler is *content with what today presents*. Reflecting on the reckless lifestyle they have chosen and the many potentially deadly or disastrous consequences they somehow escaped leaves them grateful. Today becomes a gift. What's more, being ungrateful is exhausting. There are the regrets and frustrations of yesterday always gnawing at us because of some real or perceived failures. Yesterday is relentlessly reminding us of the time and how far behind we are getting. If not the regret of yesterday, then it is the anxiety for tomorrow. The addict/criminal loves to stare at what is next. Three days clean and everyone should be on board with this troubled struggler's new game plan.

The amount of time spent aching over what happened before or fretting over what happens next leaves no energy for today and impedes gratefulness. People and events of the day become irritating because they distract the troubled strugglers from feeling sorry for themselves or taking them away from some important daydreaming. For the ungrateful, today becomes the yesterday they will regret tomorrow.

The grateful struggler *sees people in terms of relationship, not transaction*. When gratefulness takes root in the heart of the struggler, they begin to see people differently. Reflecting on their lives, they start to comprehend the indifference they have shown towards others. The guilt connected to their mistreatment of family and friends creates humility. Gratefulness is birthed when they realize that someone, anyone, still cares enough to reach out to them.

The addict/criminal on the other hand is already working an angle. The idea of "what's in it for me?" while perhaps never spoken out loud, has been a factor in most of their interactions with others. "I want what I want when I want it," lest we forget the motto of the addict/criminal.

The Art of the Spiel

Spiel (pronounced speel) — a long or fast speech or story, typically one intended as a means of persuasion or as an excuse but regarded with skepticism or contempt by those who hear it.

In their drive to satisfy whatever wants the addict/criminal can conjure up, they see others primarily as resources as opposed to people with whom they can build meaningful relationships. A good example of how the addict/criminal views people in transactional terms can be seen with those who have attempted to "help" a troubled struggler with some money.

In typical form, the addict/criminal likes to hide their activities or isolate in their addiction. Thus, the concerned parent or friend worries about their well-being. When the phone rings days, weeks, or months later or the troubled struggler shows up on their front doorstep, the obvious longing is to spend some time with them. One parent expressed that he and his wife were "hungry" for a relationship with their child.

One party is seeking a relationship, meaning mutual love and respect from one person to another, while the addict/criminal is looking for resources. The language of the ungrateful is "can you give me?" or "will you lend me?" Conversations are dominated by what "they are going through."

There is no end to the creativity of an addict/criminal. Stories of their lives become theatrical events. They can portray themselves as the unluckiest, most misunderstood and victimized creatures on earth. This comes complete with tears, graphic details, and near-death experiences, which tug at the heartstrings of "hungry" parents.

The other story, one more widely used, is one of "things going so well." This story is about the addict/criminal turning over a new leaf and getting back on track. They have a chance to go back to school. The boyfriend the parents don't trust has a chance to start a new job. Both stories end the same way with the struggler needing some money to make life work. The addict/criminal will promise to stay in touch, see you more often, call you later, or come by next weekend to help you out with a few chores. What happens next has more excuses than results.

I can think of few things more crushing than when a parent or loved one is confronted with the fact that someone they love so deeply has lied to them so convincingly. For many, this cycle goes on for years, and the parents, spouse, or friends are blinded by compassion and are used again and again.

Grateful people don't use others. They do not attach the gift of their presence as a price for others getting involved with them again. Grateful people are humbled by the fact that you came to visit them in prison. By contrast, the addict/criminal wants sex, money, food, new shoes, and any other thing he can squeeze out of the present transaction.

I can remember sitting at a table surrounded by people who, despite my long history of riotous, criminal living, extended to me another chance to be family. With the sight of food in such abundance, the aroma of which was heavenly, and kids laughing and playing, with a sense of order, I had an awareness that I belonged to something and someone. Equally as weighty was the sense of order and belonging.

At that moment it was hard to swallow my food since I was so overwhelmed with emotion — and gratitude. The thought of asking for anything more or something different would have been disgraceful. Wanting this time to end or being anxious for what's next would have been sad, and certainly, a sign that I hadn't a shred of gratitude.

Think about the conversations you have had lately with your struggler. Have they been one-sided where they tell you about all the things they miss and how you could make things a little more comfortable for them (i.e., bring them some money or food, do some laundry, watch the kids)? Perhaps they called you for the first time in weeks or months and they report that everything is going well. They have moved to a new place (their third move this year) and they and their girlfriend have new jobs. It's just so hard not having a vehicle. If they had $500, they could get the truck on the road.

One of the hardest things for me to watch is a parent or spouse who spends hundreds, sometimes thousands of dollars on a struggler to get him or her out of jail and in rehab only to have the addict/criminal call them the next week with a list of "all the things I need." The list will include cigarettes for the week, money to buy snacks, and money for a past-due phone bill so he can reach out to his girlfriend for sex or more "stuff I need."

If you find yourself the parent who is trying to explain to your addict/criminal that you just don't have the money to spend like that every week, this struggler is not humble or grateful because that is what he or she really "needs." Your answer to them should not be "I'll see what I can do," but rather, "How about you be grateful you're not in jail or on your way to prison? I think you have been given enough. It's time you realize how much your addiction is costing everyone."

I was having lunch with a gentleman once who has been on the front line of helping strugglers find their way. As we talked, we were recounting some of the challenging issues while pursuing our objective. Admitting he had made mistakes that enabled some strugglers rather than helping them (as we all have), he told me about a day that in his prayer to God he was reminded of the story in the Bible of a young man who had left home to do his own thing. In the story, this boy blew all his money and was living in squalor. Humbled by his situation, he went running home to ask his father's forgiveness.

The question occurred to this gentleman telling me this story, "What would have happened if he had been there for the boy in the story and had tried to feed and help this struggler?" His answer was that perhaps his help would have delayed what needed to happen, which was a moment of honest clarity that caused the young man to see the repercussions of his choices in life and find genuine humility leading to gratitude when his father was willing to extend grace. This is the true path to recovery and is essential for anyone who wants to take the next step. Humility and gratitude plow the hardness of our hearts to prepare the ground for new seed and a better harvest.

A Few Coins For Your Change Jar:

• There is a character blindness that occurs in our struggle. Are you willing to ask those around you if they feel you are humble and grateful?

• Do you want fairness or mercy?

• Who should decide what happens next?

CHAPTER 18

Element Three: Being Teachable

It's what you learn after you know it all that counts."
— John Wooden, Hall of Fame basketball coach

When the time comes to make some changes and not just consider the notion, you will see where your troubled struggler truly is. If you find that humility and gratitude are not at work in the life of the troubled struggler, then sadly this phase of recovery will be an exasperating, heartbreaking experience.

This phase of talking to the struggler about being responsible, however, is where many want to start when attempting to help the troubled struggler. After all, it seems practical to talk to the addict/criminal about money management when he is trying to borrow money. Why wouldn't you want to talk to the troubled struggler about their anger issues when you are on the ride home from bailing them out of jail? Addict/criminals reject responsible living because it's hard, requiring consistent discipline and time. The addict/criminal has 1,000 reasons why this is a bad idea and won't work.

Addict/criminals are professional liars. They are capable of lying with every tool available to them — they can lie with their words, their lack of words, with their actions, their tears, and their smiles. They will offer to work for "free" at your home knowing they are only buying some goodwill. They believe this will reap far more benefit for them in the long run, but it will cost you considerably more than what you would have paid a stranger to do the same job.

At this point, you may be thinking that I present a disparaging view of the addict/criminal. You must bear in mind as you read this that I have dedicated the last 20 years to helping these strugglers. While devoting my best efforts to those who are ready to be taught so they can change, I am also pragmatic about what impact I might have before they reach that point. My attempts to work harder at their recovery than the struggler themselves has proved fruitless at most every turn.

Truth is, I hate the effects of alcohol and substance abuse. I have watched it torture families, I have stood at coffins, and still hear the moans of parents who lost children to this enemy. I live with the guilt and my family bears the scars. I know what it takes to change, I have been at it for 31 years. At 25 years old, I was 6'5" and weighed 140 lbs. I had a cocaine habit that knew no limits apart from money. To spend $500 a day was not unusual. I was an angry, dangerous, selfish man who spent years in "cages." Anyone who knew me or loved me paid a price.

Yet, I had people around me who loved me, gave to me, cried for me, and even tried to talk to me. I was a professional liar; my whole life was a lie. The world was a game, everyone and everything a piece to be moved around until I could get what I wanted. The addict/criminal was me. I looked like most any kid my age. I was "married" with two beautiful kids. I managed to have a job most of the time. I was completely incognito for most people. My mother saw her little boy and was blind in some respect to the extent of my struggle.

My life began seriously descending into the abyss of addiction and the selfish, grasping lifestyle it produces. At age 30, having spent several years of my life in prison, I was once again given more prison time, 22 years to be exact. Anyone who cared did so from a distance. I remember thinking, "I have only been out of prison six months and I am headed back for a long time." Much as I hated the idea, it seemed only right to let someone in my family know I was headed back to prison. If anyone were going to take the call, it would be my oldest sister, Vic. She accepted the collect call (knowing full well what that meant), listened to my spiel, and then said these words that have stuck with me for 30 years: "Well, I hope you stay in there this time until Jesus comes back. Seems like that's the only place you do well."

Those were the exact words I needed to hear. I am so glad, looking back, that she didn't ask about what the lawyers might be saying. I am grateful she didn't talk to me about the conditions in the jail or if I needed anything. I had years to reflect on those words and this is what she said: "We've had enough."

We joke that "there is no fixing stupid," but there is. For me, Vic's words played a big part. The family was hurt and dishonored. The person I had become was no longer welcome in her life or around her family. It was obvious to her that I did not value family. I was a reckless and destructive soul, ungrateful and arrogant.

At some point, I asked God to "change my life or take my life, because I don't want to live another day like this." He did both. It started with humility. The one last "lifeline" to my life had in so many words said, "If you want to continue to live like this, I hope you live in a cage forever."

My wife was gone, kids were gone, and family done with me. I had no reputation and no money. I was nothing, had nothing, deserved nothing. It was absolutely the medicine I deserved. Emptied of all, I was able to take in some new thoughts. Slowly my behaviors started to change, slowly I began developing new habits.

Being teachable begins in moments like those. They don't have to be so tragic or drastic, but they must come. *Humble has no expectations or demands, it is surrender.* Grateful realizes there is still hope. With a heart that sets aside pride, resentment, and self-pity, the addict/criminal can now learn a new way of seeing and responding to the world.

Here are the takeaways from what I just described. The *first takeaway* is as parents or spouses of the addict/criminal, we at times will find it difficult if not impossible to watch our loved one languish in jail or experience homelessness. To enlist the help of the court system and the Marchman Act or some similar provision to order them to rehab seems unthinkable.

Addiction and the associated criminal thought process are as deadly as cancer. Chemotherapy, radiation therapy, and surgical removal are the three basic forms of treatment for cancer, all of which seem rather difficult choices. Do nothing and the patient does not get better. Comfort them and they will feel better while they die. Pretending the problem does not exist or hiding the symptoms from family members and friends would be negligent and callous.

We are often in denial and have convinced ourselves that the cancer of addiction in our child or friend is really not deadly. For most families I know, they believe the answer is to "love more, love different, give more." They believe if they just give it time, their loved one will suddenly and mysteriously grow up and all will be well.

That might be your experience, but the odds of that happening are like winning the lottery. You can play that game but be sure that the losers far outnumber the winners. No one would purposefully play a game of chance with their child or loved one, but it happens every day.

The *second takeaway* is the sooner you can help the addict/criminal reach a place of surrender, the sooner treatment can take effect. The addict/criminal may not immediately be at risk of death but the collateral damage can be worse when careers are destroyed, livelihoods robbed, children neglected or damaged, reputations ruined, legal entanglements incurred — not to mention the psychological or physical risks and damage.

If you have a loved one ready to surrender or are a criminal/addict at a place of surrender, then teachable is who they or you are. While the addict/criminal may still have opinions and may disagree with some of what they are being taught, they withhold their need to express it. The addict/criminal is starting to realize their worldview has not borne fruit. Much of what they know is tainted or colored by their addiction.

The Tourist Trap

The first lesson I share with anyone who comes into our facility is, "The only thing you need to change is everything." We begin by eliminating access to outside influence — no phone, no visits, no furloughs, no mail. The next thing they learn is that the culture of our facility is completely different from what they are used to. We monitor language and leisure activities. We insist on neatness, order, timeliness, and cleanliness. It's lights out when activities stop and sleep is valued. Lying, screaming, and threats are forbidden and have serious consequences. We emphasize respect for property, people, and one's self. I have found it helpful to use the following example to help the guys understand the logic or rationale for our actions.

If you have ever had much of a chance to travel, you discover a strange phenomenon with tourists. It seems that people tend to compare the country or state of their origin with the one they are visiting. I suppose that is understandable to some extent. What they are experiencing is a different culture; if their only reference point is the U.S., then Israel would be disorientating.

It takes a turn when Americans look for a hotel filled with other Americans. They may even look for food or amenities common to America. While sitting in the hotel dining room eating American food, they begin to complain that people treat them differently than in Georgia where they live. They are frustrated that the language is hard to understand and moan that no barbecue stands can be found.

It moves beyond that to there only being a few TV stations or that "people here drive on the wrong side of the road." They wish this foreign culture was more like America. I wonder with the cost of this vacation to a foreign land why they would want "sameness"? Why would they not want to immerse themselves in the new experience? Learn to speak the language, eat the food of that culture, listen to music, engage the locals, and learn new ideas and worldviews?

At this point, many of the guys in my facility start picking up on the parallel lesson. I ask them to look at the "cost" they paid to get to our facility, monies spent to pay the entry fees aside. I am referring to the cost to themselves, their families, kids, or spouses. Many have spent years in prison. Living a life as an addict/criminal gets expensive.

Here they are in a "foreign land" where language and culture are different and they long for sameness. They waste months, complaining about things being different than where they came from. Like the American tourist in Israel, they do not immerse themselves in the new, do not engage the locals. With a world of new opportunities surrounding them, with a chance to live and experience the new, they mope around, missing the old.

Others will discover how dependent they are on their old lifestyles; this unfamiliar new one challenges everything they understand about what makes them who they are. If it were only a matter of abstinence, how easy recovery would be. Recovery must begin with their thoughts changing, with the goal that their behaviors follow. They spend time practicing and repeating healthy behaviors until they become habits that replace the old, ultimately changing their character and who they are. The only thing that needs to change is everything, and a teachable attitude is necessary for that to happen.

A Few Coins For Your Change Jar:

- Are you teachable? Are you seeking out others to help you learn or are you fighting those who try?

- How much time are you committing to classes, reading or, instruction?

- What areas do you need the most help right now to learn?

CHAPTER 19

Element Four: Being Accountable

"You will not experience dramatic change in your struggle as long as you use accountability to describe your sins instead of declaring your need for help in the midst of temptation."— Heath Lambert, Finally Free: Fighting for Purity with the Power of Grace

The next rung on the ladder of recovery is accountability. I might argue this is the most important step because the life of an addict/criminal is often one of secrets and deceit. The struggler can be surrounded by people who do not know them or exist isolated even within their small band of addict cohorts.

The heartbreaking fact that an addict/criminal can overdose and not be missed for hours or even days is only surpassed by the struggler who lives among us and goes without being called out. The addict/criminal who abuses the caring people in his or her life, while those abused strugglers remain mostly silent or paralyzed, unable to take action.

The model for anyone who wishes to see an addict/ criminal out of the darkness involves three steps: *direct, redirect, self-direct.* The struggler will always default to self-direct mode. If there is to be a legitimate shift towards true self-direction, it will begin with the addict/criminal becoming accountable to someone else. Accountability to others is a foreign concept and being honest is one of the hardest things they will ever be asked to do.

Daily phone calls, weekly meetings, saving receipts and budgeting, and honest, impactful conversations where someone of influence will ask the hard questions are where accountability starts. It can't be like pulling teeth. The addict/criminal will agree to such account-ability only to make the process torturous to those brave or patient enough to get involved at this stage. The idea prevails that they can outlast you until you surrender, allowing them to slide back under the shroud of secrets and deceit.

Another common tactic used by the addict/criminal is to use the term "to be honest with you." Have you ever been talking to your struggling loved one when "I am going to be honest with you" becomes the preface to an answer? Smile and ask them if that means everything they have said up to that point has been dishonest. More importantly, submit whatever comes next to intense scru-tiny.

Addict/criminals like to "softball," which is my slang for those who give me *a* truth when I was looking for *the* truth. Let me give you an example. I am talking to my addict struggler and I ask, "What was your biggest struggle this week?" Their head goes down for a moment, then looking up with an intense look in their eyes from what appears to be painful memories, they say, "I want to be honest with you. I thought about going into the bar Wednesday evening, I even pulled in the parking lot and sat there staring at the front door, but then I remembered I was supposed to meet Brian for a meeting downtown. So I just left and went straight there."

Now what they said may or may not have had any basis in reality but what they did was throw me a softball. Their real struggle was resentment at work because they don't make enough money and child support is drowning them. They are lonely, considered calling a girl they met at one of the meetings that would probably sleep with them, but instead resorted to porn. They gave me *a* truth but not *the* truth.

Accountability is a process established over time and affects every aspect of life. It restores dignity and trust. I cannot overemphasize the importance of getting planted in the recovery community. I use that term about as broadly as it can be used because I believe that recovery varies for different people. That does not give credence to the struggler who rejects accountability and declares his recovery does not include the community. The absence of disclosure, lack of receptivity, and absence of self-criticism are textbook criminal thinking.

The recovery community is a term used specifically to describe the many "anonymous" type meetings — alcohol anon, narcotics anon, meetings, or "the rooms" as they are often referred to. However, when I use the term community, it has far broader implications. I believe in AA and NA and all their cousins. I believe the church can meet the need for being planted in community as well. Several faith-based 12-step groups are equally as effective in developing accountability and new social networking.

I will always prefer a group that addresses the three parts of mankind: body, soul, and spirit. I find this practice most prevalent in the faith-based community. Church plus Celebrate Recovery is a near-perfect formula, in my opinion, but everyone won't go that path as they have issues with Christianity, "organized religion," or God as described in the Bible.

Community brings about accountability. Community is made up of families who, when there is an empty seat at the table, have someone picking up the phone to see where their loved one is. Every week at five you show up at the meeting except tonight and people start asking if anyone has heard from you. Becoming part of the recovery family is crucial. It exponentially multiplies success in the battle against the addict/criminal mindset.

We will talk about what relapse looks like in a later chapter but know this: Isolation is the enemy of wholeness. "It is not good that man should be alone" was not written just to encourage marriage; it is a universal principle relevant to many situations. The addict/criminal struggling to be set free will either find a group of people to network with that encourage wholeness and push them forward in the struggle, or they will gravitate back to the comfort of dysfunctional relationships.

Accountability is in essence the knowledge on the part of the struggler that they alone not only do not have the solution but in fact, will become the problem. They welcome the light of being known; they know it may well be life or death. They relish the strength of being in a family.

This is the most important transition of going from what I know to what I do — a willingness to be vulnerable and exposed. Teaching now gets tied to criticism, oversight, and correction. It leads to rules borne out of healthy relationships. We create and cultivate levels of protective, nurturing influences and relationships. For many this becomes too painful, while others fall into years of deception, feigning accountability.

A Few Coins For Your Change Jar:

- Where are you being seen by others?

- Is your schedule so full of stuff it doesn't include real relationships? Who is asking you the tough questions?

- Is there anyone in your life that you can tell anything to, without fear of judgment?

CHAPTER 20

Element Five:
Being Responsible

"In terms of responsibility, there are only
two choices: make it happen or make excuses."
– Jim Adkins, author of Monsters and Butterflies

When all is said and done, isn't this what we want for ourselves and those we love and care for — to live responsibly? It is being surrounded by healthy relationships, equipped with truth that gives context to life, planted in a family that provides belonging and loving support. Then we are no longer struggling to be free but are free to struggle in a safe environment.

Life threw some curveballs, people have done damage, or circumstances were not always favorable. What would have been our excuses for being less now drive us to be more. Too long have I let life and others define me, too long have I lived for myself apart from others.

I have worked hard, paid dearly, and my limp is not my shame; it is proof of my ability to survive. I have no delusions about how I got here — grace and family. Family, that community of people who keep me in place, hold me accountable to a standard that provides protection and the ability to flourish.

Directed, redirected, and now self-directed, I become co-director of this recovery program called life. I find pleasure and help in daily maintenance, unwavering commitment to the path, brutal honesty, humble acceptance of criticism from those that care for me, self-discipline, self-affirmation, self-motivation, and cultivation of the community in which I have found peace and order.

Fiercely independent people are an anomaly, not a goal to be sought after. Healthy dependence on others is in the design of the Almighty. In the beginning, God started by creating relationships. All of nature is tied together through remarkable interdependence. Science, if it has proven anything, is the proof of dependence and relationship.

Responsible people have invested in the hard work of change and they prove it by their actions. The addict/criminal in contrast would like to sell the language of "responsible" like a used car salesman. Talk is their currency. They believe that if they remain "trouble-free" and "clean" for 90 days, others should consider them responsible. The criminal/addict has thrived on immediate gratification. He will not accept that responsible living requires time, patience, self-discipline.

Responsible people are not perfect and they know it. Knowing this, they are prepared. In my book *Monsters and Butterflies*, I talked about planning to fail. The idea is that while I take steps to create and cultivate a future, I surround myself with a network of people and resources to encourage and protect me. Failure then does not become fatal.

During a discussion with others on leadership, I picked up this line that has stuck with me: "If you are constantly telling people you are the boss, you're probably not." I think that works as well with being responsible; when you are responsible you won't have to convince anyone.

Jimmy D

Jimmy D was an angry young man when he walked through the doors. He wasn't in humble mode but he was getting there. Conflicted is the state in which I find most strugglers, and Jimmy was tired of losing but in love with risk. Strugglers like Jimmy love their kids but are ignorant of fatherhood. They demand respect but are unable to give it; willing to change things but rarely changing themselves.

That was the case with Jimmy D — warm tears one day, scorching tongue the next. He was one of those guys with whom we just weren't sure what to expect. A hardcore druggie and criminal, he had been a supervisor and a father — but was conflicted.

Jimmy did the next right thing to change. He acted as if he had adopted some different coping skills, not without kicking and screaming mind you, but just kept plugging. He also made a couple of really good choices. One, he did not give up but decided to rely on fact not feeling. Two, he got involved in the recovery community. He stuck to a job for some time gaining influence and trust.

This, in concert with his networking in the community, built his reputation, trust, and confidence. He was reliable, prompt, and prepared and when he stumbled, there were dozens of arms to hold him in place. Today he is a "rock star" in the community, a giving, caring, hardworking man. Responsible is a word anyone who knows Jimmy would attribute to him. Four years clean, I am so proud of this guy. I have almost forgotten all the times he cussed me out.

Some might see my friend on the "road to recovery" and their focus fall on the scars on his arms or the scrapes on his knees where he has fallen. I see the direction his eyes are facing. I see the ground he has covered, the fact that he is up and walking. I know he deals with pain, disappointment, rejection, guilt, and remorse — but he's dealing with it. He's responsible.

Where are you in the process? Where is your loved one, the struggling addict/criminal? Can you go back over the material in what recovery looks like and find this person or yourself? If you are a struggling addict/criminal, do you dare hear the assessment of those who know you, of where you might be in the process?

I want to take a few pages to talk about relapse, the subtle process by which we turn away from recovery. You may think it's a dramatic moment when a struggler wakes up and decides to "leave the ranch," but it is not. It was brewing and growing inside for a while. While looking at relapse, we will also take a look into the heart and mind of the addict/criminal. If at the end of my relapse discussion, you find that the troubled struggler you are trying to help looks more like relapse than recovery, then it is time to be honest about what happens next.

Humble – Grateful – Teachable – Accountable – Responsible. Remember the allegory of the watch. You or your struggler do not get to decide what piece goes in where or when.

A Few Coins For Your Change Jar:

- Most people can point to five things that have keep them clean while in rehab or while in recovery. List at least five.

Example:

1. Submitting to accountability to other people about my life

2. UA or BA testing

3. Attending meetings

4. Avoiding trigger people or trigger places

5. Coping skills for dealing with stressors

6. Community/phone numbers

- Responsibility says: I get to be Co-Director of my program, how many of these am I using?

CHAPTER 21

Self Diagnosis

*"Rarely do I truly understand the disease which
ails me. Therefore, rarely do I truly understand
the fix that would cure me. And so maybe I should
truly contemplate how rarely I recognize that God
understands both." — Craig D. Jonesborough, Author*

The prognosis is positive, the treatment on track. Then, however, a new doctor takes over the case, and his name is Dr. Addict. Dr. Addict decides that the treatment is too costly, basically ineffective, or worse, concludes that the patient is cured. This will usually be preceded with the oft-repeated, always-fatal phrase, "All I need is ..."

This is a definite warning sign; the gauge is showing a dangerous direction. It's been a few meetings since Sara showed up. She does not return text messages, so Mia decides to stop by and check on her friend. The story she gets is not a new one. "I'm so busy with my job and my kid. *I don't think I need* to go to a meeting all the time."

For a moment forget the circumstances, the logistics of juggling a job and kids. it's the line *"I don't think I need"* that should cause the red lights to start flashing. If you hear yourself making those types of declarations, you have begun to speak the language of relapse.

Relapse sneaks in the back door, thief that it is. The path to relapse can be a sudden event, with extreme stressors and a failed support system triggered by some tragic event. More often than not, however, relapse has a subtle slide. Because we have developed negative habits and coping mechanisms in response to our challenges after years of abuse, it requires nothing more than becoming passive in our recovery to begin the descent of relapse.

Addict/criminals in their pride can become their own doctor, prescribing the remedy for their ills. They will even do so shamelessly from a jail cell, while in rehab, or from a hospital bed. I want to counter some of the typical arguments from the addict/criminal as they attempt to self-diagnose, much as I might if I were in a one-on-one with an individual. Every response will be a little different, but my talking points remain the same. When I respond to the arguments, I am redirecting the conversation to cover a set of bullet points I will list below.

My Responses

Sitting across from me is a struggler who's wrestling with the idea that perhaps he needs to be in counseling as it appears his lifestyle is taking some dark turns. That is when Dr. Addict shows up. "All I need is to get a job and pay off some of my fines," the doctor says.

"Haven't you had some really good jobs already? The problem is not getting a job; it's being able to keep the job. Someone much smarter than

I, said you can't solve problems with the same answers that got you into the mess to start with."

Again, this struggling young lady trying to make sense of her situation says, "Everything went bad when he walked out on me."

"I know that it was devastating when he left you to fend for yourself. I know how hurtful it is to be betrayed. The world can be a really tough place sometimes. Sadly, it was you who was driving when you got the DUI. Your drinking is making things so much worse. You are trying to cope with real pain by using a method that has proven deadly many times over."

"I don't need a sermon."

"No, you don't and I don't have one for you but I believe you know it's truth and accountability that you don't want to face right now, which is something you need if you are ever going to get your life on track."

Has anyone heard this line from your struggling loved one? "*I just need* to borrow some money?" Probably more than a few have. My answer would be something like this:

"Man, if it was really that simple. We've been giving you money and helping you for years and here we are again. We haven't advanced any real change in the way you manage your life. What you need is to admit this isn't working, because that is what your mom and I realized. We want to help you, but this isn't how."

"You have never been an addict. You can't possibly know what it feels like. How are you going help me?"

"I don't need to be an addict to see that you need to be surrounded by some people who cannot only walk with you through a detox program but walk with you through life. There is a life apart from drugs and alcohol, but no one gets there alone. I can help you find those people."

I utilize some basic talking points when I answer the arguments and self-diagnosis, I am redirecting the conversation to reflect the bullet points below.

a) "Do what you did, get what you got." You can't expect new results with old responses (more money, another job). Instead, new thinking about life is the remedy.

b) What is your role in this mess? (Stop shifting the blame.)

c) You really don't know what is needed or we wouldn't be having this conversation. You are acting as Dr. Addict.

d) Certain answers in life transcend or rise above the circumstances.

A Case Study

Let me share with you a case. I have changed the names and some of the characters out of respect for the privacy of those involved. Eric was 60 years old and college educated, and had held some good jobs in his lifetime. He was married with adult children when I met him. Eric was an alcoholic and had been for many years. When we met, he had lost jobs, his wife, reputation and was living with his elderly father, living on his dad's social security.

Dad knew and admitted he was an enabler, but just couldn't say no to his son. He finally convinced Eric to go into detox and from there to complete an in-house drug rehab program in Georgia. Eric did so without incident, attended all classes, was a gentleman by and large, and did not represent any issues according to the rehab staff.

About six months into the program, Eric, unbeknownst to anyone except Dad, started to plan his premature exit. Eric convinced his estranged wife that he was "better than ever and would never return to the lifestyle of a drunk" so she agreed to reunite with him. Secretly he assured his family that he had "learned all he was going to get from this program" and went on to explain that "getting back to work was imperative."

It's important to note that no one from the family called to express concerns over the recent changes, and his decision to leave rehab early was not seen by his family as a typical addict/criminal response. It was a fatal mistake, however, and within days after leaving, he had moved with a "friend" into the woods in a neighboring state. Within a few months, we got the call that he had died in a collision while intoxicated.

I am always shocked by the news of a death like this. I called Eric on the day he was leaving the rehab and asked him to reconsider. I wanted to speak with his dad who was there to pick him up, but Eric refused. Eric convinced himself and his family that in the face of counsel from doctors, trained professional counselors, legal counsel, the "Big Book" of AA, his sponsor, his home group, and those in the rehab with him, he was not making a big mistake. He maintained that he was the one who had the best "prescription" for his life.

Eric was at the place in rehab where a transformative change may have taken place. The "lines had been drawn with his addiction." He could have leaned on his support group and pushed into a new reality of sobriety as a lifestyle, but It would have required that those closest to him be able to see the warning signs of self-diagnosis.

The addict/criminal needed to be warned at that moment when the gauges of his life started to spin and the lights flashed red. I will refer back to this case as we watch the progression of relapse unfold. It is also important to note that this man was in a rehab "playing by the rules" but was never fully engaged, and never in recovery — the signs were there. I want you to see the signs and not ignore, excuse, or hide them.

One last thought about my experience with the alcoholic mindset. The addict/criminal who by and large is "just a drinker" loves isolation. They will go to work, and after work stop and grab a 12-pack on the way home and pass out while watching TV. Then they progress to an 18-pack over the years. Sadly, no one may do or say much until the struggler has a tragic car accident or gets arrested for DUI — or their liver goes kaput.

Isolation is anti-accountability. This type of struggler becomes furious if others expose their addiction, will demand "privacy," and can be even worse when their criminal thinking prevails. They are often abusive, withhold financial support, threaten, and demean. They are manipulative beyond words.

The fact that their drug is legal engenders an irrational view that they are "not doing anything wrong."

Blame-shifting and resentments validate the anger in their deluded minds. Any harm done can be paid for with gifts or smoothed over with empty platitudes. They are a special kind of sick.

If your troubled struggler has begun prescribing for him or her self "what they need," if their life choices fly in the face of good counsel, know they have begun the descent down the ladder towards relapse.

A Few Coins For Your Change Jar:

- One of the hardest things to grapple with is that our best decisions landed us in addiction. Am I really the doctor I need right now?

- Have you been neglecting good counsel because you don't think you need their advice?

- Does your struggling loved one find fault with "the program" that has been holding their life in place?

CHAPTER 22

Romanticizing

*"I used to tell stories of my addiction as though it
was a script from some hilarious comedy movie.
When the lights came on, I realized the gravity
of my behavior on others, others who did not
deserve such disrespect and victimization.
The laughing stopped." — Jim Adkins*

Romanticizing is the ability of the addict/criminal
to selectively remember or perhaps conveniently
forget the entirety of the "stories of their lives." We like
to say that the addict/criminal only "plays the highlight
reel." Our former life gets reduced to moments. Rationale is replaced by rationalization. Our issues from the
past are referred to as mistakes. We remember the fun,
thrill, and rush while suppressing the shame and self-ha-
tred we felt in the aftermath.

To talk the language of relapse is to "brag about our
escapades." The stories are told with great humor. One
individual was recounting his getting stuck in a pickup
truck loaded with copper after he had used an axe to

remove copper grounding cables from phone poles. The whole room laughed at this ridiculous moment.

I asked my class if they remembered that there was a mother who woke up that same evening to find her child not breathing but when she attempted to call an ambulance for the baby, her phone and those of her neighbors on that street had been disrupted — and that child had died.

The class was silent, heads lowered, and the young man who was telling the story had his eyes water up in shame. Romanticizing our lives as an addict/criminal is a sign — first that we are not in recovery, and second that we are moving into a dangerous place with our life, a sure indication relapse is taking hold. I tell you these things as a warning that must not be ignored. Use it to assess the loved one who is struggling. An aspect of romanticizing is often referred to as *minimalization,* which is the fascinating habit of reducing the impact or severity of behaviors by the addict/criminal.

I was at a meeting with a large group of people, many I did not know personally, and was only introduced as I was seated for the afternoon meeting. As we were introduced by name only, it was purely by coincidence that a conversation began about a crime recently committed. The lady who recounted the story explained that she and her daughter had walked into their home and immediately smelled cigarette smoke. As no one in this home was a smoker, they froze in the front room, across the room from a door that led into an area where the door was always closed when it was not in use.

On this particular day, the door was open, revealing a sliding closet door partially open as well. The lady telling the story was certain that an intruder was behind that closed door. The lady and her daughter fled the home and called the police. While it was discovered that someone had burglarized this home, no one was apprehended. They were then afraid to be in their own home, traumatized by this encounter. Their lives were forever changed.

I was sick to my stomach; I felt the lightheadedness of one struck by a tragic loss. Having committed these types of burglaries as a young man while an addict/criminal, never once had the impact of my actions come home to me in this way. Under the influence of my addiction and criminal thought process, I had excused my behavior as youthful indiscretion. I was proud of the fact I had not "victimized" the innocent like bank tellers or store clerks. The homes I had entered were "empty." I am guilty to the grave for these behaviors and I cannot be sorry enough to undo the damage even 40 years later.

Many who engage in romanticizing see certain traits of their addiction or criminality as trivial or inconsequential. They will postulate that alcohol and marijuana use were "never the problem." Another such presumption is that their crimes were "petty" when compared to others. I like to call it "playing the Hitler card." ("At least I'm not like Hitler.") It is that absurd and sick.

Can you see the slide starting to take place? Here is the conversation that is rattling around in the head of the addict/criminal: *"I am feeling better, and the longer I stay in treatment, the farther behind I am getting. I need to get out there and take care of business. Sure, I made some stupid mistakes, but I need to move on. My girl and I have had some fun times. I just need to take my life more seriously."*

Alarms should be blaring when we hear that conversation or train of thought. We need to slow that train to a stop because it is surely headed for an accident. If not, I weep for the passengers and those on the tracks ahead.

A Few Coins For Your Change Jar:

- Which is more accurate about your life; I made some mistakes in my life, or I victimized and abused others and myself?

- When you talk to your struggling addict/criminal do you hear phrases like, "I don't know why you are making such a big deal over _____ "?

- How do you retell the stories of your life? Do you tell the whole story?

CHAPTER 23

Victim/Villain

"Victimhood gives us great moral superiority and entitles us to unquestioning sympathy while exempting us from examining any single one of our actions. A victim is utterly devoid of responsibility or blame." — Belinda Brown

As director of a restoration house a few years back, I routinely sat down with every new resident and talked about expectations and a host of other things. After some time, I gave them a sealed envelope marked "do not open." I told them that at a certain point during their stay we would sit down and open it together and when we did, they would think I was a prophet.

The letter inside was a series of statements that almost without exception would prove true. I am certainly no prophet but, having worked with men in addiction for so long, I knew at some point we would need to challenge some conclusions and assumptions with which the addict/criminal seems to struggle.

At the beginning of their transition from the extreme confines of a jail or prison cell to the far less stringent environment of our home, the struggler is filled with hope, "ready to get started in the program" and is usually grateful and cooperative. However, the insidious nature of addiction rarely "tempts" the struggler with a frontal attack. In other words, our addiction will rarely say to us, "Let's go shoot heroin."

Instead, it will begin by pointing out difficult areas of the program that are "unfair" or "unreasonable." This redirects the focus of the struggler to what can be used to justify why they are feeling like walking away from the process. It now becomes like a "scale" where we weigh in our hearts the reasons to quit versus the reasons to stick it out.

If this phenomenon is not recognized and called out, the struggler like Eric reaches a tipping point and loses his or her ability to be humble, grateful, or teachable. We start hearing a new language that is colored with dissent and questions about fairness or worth. That's the deceptive language of addiction. The struggler is being "painted" as a victim by the program. The program is vilified as insincere, unfair, or guilty of ulterior motives. "They just want my money; they aren't really teaching me anything; I'm not getting anywhere; this is a waste of time."

This is when I ask the resident to break out the envelope. Inside are the very words I am writing to you right now. In a nutshell, I have written "Why am I here? I don't think this is helping. I feel like leaving." Hopefully, the struggler will realize his addiction is screaming for him to return to the dark dysfunction of his former lifestyle. It is a ploy to get them "alone," angry, and disillusioned.

Self-deception and passivity have a price and it is blindness. The disease of responsibility shifting has set in. Others are now seen as hypocrites. They are selfish and "obviously have some problems." We feel misunderstood, mistreated, and worse, lied to. The program is BS and for this, we have abandoned our old friends who at least understood us. Counsel meant to protect us is now seen as judgment. It is the "old 80/20 syndrome."

The 80/20 Syndrome

I don't know the statistics and don't even want to. I know it happens way too often and when it does, it crushes hearts. It often happens unexpectedly and when it does, it tears at the fabric of our communities and nation. It may be part of your story. A married man of 20 or so years comes home and declares to the family that he is leaving. I just chose 20 years; it could be five years but it doesn't matter. The effect is still the same. What happened? Many admit they didn't even realize there was a problem with the marriage until someone walked out.

I am using the husband in this story but it could just as easily be the wife. It has been some years since the honeymoon, more than that since the dating. Passivity sets in, normal becomes too normal, and little or no effort is put into keeping the marriage light glowing. The simple fact is that life is not a nonstop vacation or honeymoon; it is fast paced. People work too much, are not connected at a soul level. We race through the years with a few memorable moments to which we can cling. There are children, bills, and a variety of problems that demand our attention while our marriage gets taken for granted.

The new lady at the job is young and friendly and she goes out of her way to speak to the boss every day.

The boss finds it refreshing to have a new face and fun conversation, and he is around her eight to ten hours a day. At first, they become friends, then they start feeling an attraction, then the 80/20 syndrome kicks in!

It has been years since he laughed and talked with a female the way she smiles at him and makes sure he has coffee or is anxious to help. His wife hasn't really "shown any interest" in his work in years, but this new lady thinks the boss is a genius. His wife has aged, given birth to four children, and gained a few pounds. Skinny jeans and a low-cut blouse have been replaced with jogging pants and a t-shirt. When the man comes home, it is the kids yelling and his wife says, "Bye, I have to take Chrissy to her softball game." That means Dad has the other three for the evening. When Mom comes home, there is an argument because Dad is asleep in his chair and their son has yet to do his homework.

He goes into work the next day and there is the "new lady." She greets him with a smile, hands him a cup of coffee, and says, "I want to show you the report from yesterday." Smelling like heaven, she leans over the desk to point out some figures he might want to consider. The only figure he is thinking about is the one so close she is brushing up against him. And just like that, the trap door opens and another victim of the 80/20 syndrome falls. Everyone he knows, who was counting on him for love and security, falls with him. Character, like a book, takes years to write, but only seconds to burn.

The problem is that he traded 80 percent of what was good in his relationship, for the 20 percent he felt he was missing. Instead of looking at the 80 percent — how his wife has helped him build the business, how she sacrificed a career to raise their children and "be there" for them every day. She worked hard at keeping the house nice, keeping his clothes clean and suits pressed. This man had lost focus, he had neglected to invest in the marriage, he chose to blame shift and justify his actions on how he was misunderstood, he was a victim of neglect, he wasn't being treated fairly.

Then came the "new lady." But it doesn't have to be a person; it could be new money, a new job, a new opportunity. The 80/20 syndrome is responsible for many a struggler walking away from recovery. When you stop looking at what your homegroup of NA or Celebrate Recovery has done to bring you into this new way of sober living, you instead start complaining about who runs the meeting, how long it lasts, or how boring the meetings are becoming — 80/20.

When rehab becomes "a stupid program, all we do is go over the same stuff, my sponsor isn't all that, he has problems too so how's he going to tell me I am wrong," then we meet Rachel at the meeting. She wants to hang out at her place. After hanging with her for a while, it gets harder and harder to say goodbye. Soon we are skipping meetings just to be together. When someone at the rehab suggests there might be an issue with co-dependence or danger to your recovery in such an early stage, 80/20 kicks in and we start "making a mental list" of how we are being mistreated vs. "whatever help" I might be getting — 80/20.

The victim/villain stage is critical in the relapse process. Do you see how this is all tying together? As parents or caregivers to the struggler, do you hear the language of the various steps of the ladder that lead to relapse? It happens every day, in rehabs everywhere. It happens in 12-step meetings, in churches, marriages, and jobs.

The 80/20 syndrome takes our eyes off the things that have been holding our life together (80%) and points to the things we are being asked to forgo right now (20%). That's how we roll as an addict/criminal. We want what we want when we want it. If only we knew that the next stage is what I call "death row," as discussed in the next chapter.

A Few Coins For Your Change Jar:

- Do you get the 80/20 syndrome? Where is it trying to creep in to your life?

- Evaluate, or better yet, ask someone else to evaluate your daily conversation for the red flags of Self-Diagnosis, Romanticizing or Victim/Villain thinking.

- Warning: These are not cute chapters in a book. If you or your loved one are exhibiting these behaviors, *seek help now.*

CHAPTER 24

Isolation

"It begins with isolation — demons always inhabit desolate places." — John Geddes

Hurting, angry, lonely, tired are the words that make up the acronym HALT. We use this to talk to men about the times in their day or life when they are vulnerable to the siren call of their addiction. It is at these moments that we need community by attending a meeting or calling a sponsor or friend who can walk us out of that dark "neighborhood." Our addiction has been setting us up the whole time. It is "cunning and baffling." We have been setting ourselves up. Let's just quickly review how we got here.

First, we "took charge" of our case. After all, who better than the addict/criminal to speak to the needs of the addict/criminal? Next, we reminded ourselves of all the fun we had running wild and partying. *We play hours of highlight reels in our mind.* We contacted some girls from our past on Facebook and started kicking it with them. Our problem, we diagnose, was all the "hard drugs." If I just stick to beer and a little weed, it will be fine.

Slowly the focus changes and we start to "see" how everyone is trying to run our lives. After all, we have been "clean" for months now. We "see" where we are only getting "farther behind in life." We "see" the hypocrisy of all these people who say they are trying to help. The answer to our ills? "I need to get away and figure some things out." The stage is set and we are under attack. Getting "back to my life" is now an imperative. We embrace a false sense of bravado. "I don't need anyone telling me how to live. I have always been able to figure things out."

Isolation is not necessarily about solitude. Solitude is a necessary place to go when it comes to thinking through life's challenges. Isolation is when we move away from the people and community that can speak life into us. It is separation from accountability. The reality of isolation is that it can take place in a room full of people. We can have a good job and still be moving towards isolation. We can be married with kids, sit in a church, go to family gatherings, and still isolate. Isolation from accountability is the issue. We know hundreds of people, but no one knows us.

Isolation and mental health go hand in hand. I know that some people reading this just recoiled emotionally if not physically when I brought up mental health. I have watched men in transitional phase interviews who, when asked about their physical health needs, would laugh or quickly respond much the same way. They would invariably talk about working out or exercising, diet, smoking, or some such bad habit they could eliminate or regulate.

The next question would be what mental health needs do you have? Their answer was silence, the question repeated out loud gained an awkward look on their faces in return. Painfully they would say, "Keep taking my medicine." More times than not they would say, "I think I'm getting pretty good in that area. I don't feel I have mental health issues."

The stigma attached to talking about mental health is widespread. It has been associated with insanity or disorder to the degree that no one wants to "label" themselves or be labeled. I understand the discomfort of such a moment. As one who holds to a tripartite view of mankind (body, soul, spirit), I have found that the same answer can be true if asked about my physical, mental, or spiritual "needs." I need to exercise more, adjust my diet, live a more balanced life, and replace some bad habits with some healthier ones.

Regarding my mental health particularly, I recognize that if the other areas are not being addressed, it will affect how I feel, my ability to concentrate and sleep, my energy levels, and mental balance. Eating right is not just a physical health need but a mental health one. Sleeping well is a mental health need. Tuning out of the noise from TV, radio, talking, traffic, so I can listen to my thoughts, question myself, challenge my assumptions — those are all mental health needs.

Like exercise, it starts slowly and uncomfortably. It requires discipline and personal initiative to establish a routine. What the heck does all that have to do with isolation? Everything! People like me tend to isolate, not because we don't like people, but because we like quiet. I can be prideful by not wanting to ask for help or for that matter even discuss my struggles. I must exercise that "muscle."

Community is a good thing in so many ways. Relationships are what the world was created for. History, literature, sociology, and psychology all attest to the value of community. I purposefully engage with men every week. It is an exercise in my mental health regimen. I am not particularly social, but I'm learning, practicing, and I am in a war with isolation because I have watched how that practice kills.

I call isolation "death row." When you isolate, you have sentenced yourself to death and "the day" will come. You may not die physically for years and years, but opportunity dies, meaningful relationships die, growth as a balanced person dies. Just like death row, you are not dead, but you are sitting there waiting. The sad part is that isolation is self-imposed. As an addict/criminal, we think we are invincible, we "don't need nobody" and are a one-man machine. We are deceived. We need rescuing or we are headed for a relapse.

If as a parent, caregiver, or loved one of someone angry and isolated, I grieve for you if your addict/criminal is isolating. Seek help, impose on this struggler, risk their anger, risk their insults. Do not validate or enable in any way this stage they have chosen. Care enough to speak to this deception. There is only one ingredient left before relapse is guaranteed and sadly it is common to us all.

A Few Coins For Your Change Jar:

- Discuss what you think it means that "it is not good that man should be alone."

- Who *really knows* you?

- Have you placed yourself on "Death Row"? The door is not locked, you know.

CHAPTER 25

Stressors

*"If you really want to escape the things that
harass you, what you're needing is not to be in
a different place but to be a different person."*
— Lucius Annaeus Seneca, Letters from a Stoic

*"Toxic relationships are dangerous to your health; they
will literally kill you. Stress shortens your lifespan.
Even a broken heart can kill you. There is an undeniable
mind-body (soul) connection. Your arguments and
hateful talk can land you in the emergency room or in the
morgue. You were not meant to live in a fever of anxiety;
screaming yourself hoarse in a frenzy of dreadful, panicked
fight-or-flight that leaves you exhausted and numb with
grief. You were not meant to live like animals tearing one
another to shreds. Don't turn your hair gray. Don't carve
a roadmap of pain into the sweet wrinkles on your face.
Don't lay in the quiet with your heart pounding like a
trapped, frightened creature. For your own precious
and beautiful life, and for those around you — seek help or
get out before it is too late. This is your wake-up call!"*
— Bryant McGill

The process has spiraled downward. From the
moment Dr. Addict took the case, it has been one

misdiagnosis after another. The treatment plan is a failed mess. The attempts to cover up the illness have only led to further spreading. He has prescribed anger, deception, denial, blame-shifting, lying, and keeping secrets to adjust for the "dis-ease" of living the addict/criminal lifestyle. All the gauges on our train are spinning, alarms screaming and lights flashing, but they have all been ignored and silenced as we isolate from those who might be able to reach out to us and for us. Our lives are racing down the track, and no one is prepared for the danger ahead.

It's true. You can be sober and still act like an addict/criminal. You are not dealing with your anger issues; in fact, it only makes you angrier to have someone bring it up to you. So, why is it a surprise when those you love walk out on you and your response is outrage? Your life is so out of balance that there is no longer a disciplined routine. Alone and angry, you plow through each day, starving your spiritual life, damaging your mental health, paying the price with your physical health.

The boss is riding you for coming in late twice this week, your work ethic is suffering because you are on the phone constantly trying to yell your wife and kid back into your life. Your answer is sex with the girl you met at the casino you decided was wise to go to. She had an STD, so now you are sitting in the urgent care facility instead of at work. Little do you know your boss has had enough. As you sit there scratching off lotto tickets you bought with money you couldn't afford to spend, a wave of stressors is rising like a tsunami over your head.

How's that for a story with some stressors? Right now, moms and dads everywhere are shaking their heads in disbelief and mild embarrassment. At the same time, there are sons everywhere hoping I don't get this book into their parents' hands. Stressors can be a million things to a million people. They are a fact of life — things break, relationships need maintenance, bills start piling up

For our part, we find our addict/criminal angry, alone, too proud to admit their failure with guilt rising and bills piling up. Now our addiction has us right where it has wanted us since the day we thought about getting clean. We are vulnerable to every trigger; we fight and fight but then we fall. The tendency to point to a specific trigger as the "the reason" we relapsed is irrational. Just like in the metaphor of the train wreck I described earlier, this has been a long time coming. This is not a surprise to anyone aware of the warning signs:

1. "I know what I need; you don't know me; just because I use doesn't make me an addict;"

2. Hangs out with addict/criminals — gone for hours or days;

3. Sleeps in, misses work;

4. Angry, not open to conversation;

5. Drops out of treatment or stops attending meetings;

6. Moves out, quits job, leaves school, stops calling;

7. In debt, the spouse leaves, or the struggler gets arrested.

The progression of these events can be incremental for years or happen relatively quickly. The important thing is to be aware and not ignore the flashing lights and tracking gauges. A ladder is a metaphor to help us look at relapse. It is not an exact science, but this is the bottom rung.

The nature of these last few chapters is disheartening. Having watched this deadly process play out multiple times can make a man like me question my calling. I love the addict/criminal. I understand them intimately. Relapse is quite common, but that doesn't make it any less serious. In the next few chapters, I will be giving you some detailed steps on how to flourish in your recovery and how to create and cultivate a lifestyle that sustains and enriches you and those around you.

A Few Coins For Your Change Jar:

- What stressors are overwhelming you?

- How many of these stressors are self-imposed and could be changed with some help?

- What is stopping me from reaching out for help?

CHAPTER 26

The Formula

"Our dilemma is that we hate change and love it at the same time; what we really want is for things to remain the same but get better." —Sydney J Harris

My question to every audience I have had the privilege of speaking with is the same. "Do *you* want to change, or do you just want *things* to be different?" We all want some things to be different, right? I haven't met anyone who is completely satisfied with their life or life habits. Changing things is the easy part. If you don't believe me ask the struggler in your life. The addict/criminal is renowned for changing stuff. We change jobs four or five times a year. We change where we live on a whim. She has a different boyfriend every time you run into her. We change geography and think we are going to make a new start. The problem is that wherever we go there we are.

In my book *Monsters and Butterflies*, I spoke in depth about the process of change, specifically transformation, which is a metamorphosis of the heart, the kind that encompasses the entire man. The formula is still the same: thoughts, behavior, habits, character. That is how we became an addict/criminal — the downward descent into our struggles.

Pray For Chris

The sun was just starting to peak at the edge of the morning as I drove to work. I was taking my usual route to the rehab center where I served as a facility coordinator. My truck was probably traveling at 45 mph on a near-dark stretch of road in rural Florida. That's when I saw the body. How I did, I'm not sure to this day. It was just a glance, but I was certain I had seen a body lying in the grass at a crossroads. I took the next chance to turn my truck around, trying to convince myself it was an animal and not really a body.

As I approached where I believed I had seen the body, I pulled my truck off the road and set out on foot. That's when I smelled a rank odor, and I realized that the body was, in fact, a body. There in the weeds in the fetal position was the outline of what appeared to be a young man. I say appeared, since I was still several yards away but I could see the body was partially clothed and covered with flies. I froze, thinking this was perhaps the scene of a crime. There was a phone and some other items scattered near the body.

I called 911 and spoke with an operator who asked me the obvious questions. The one I wasn't expecting was when she asked, "Is he breathing?" I told her the body was swarming with flies and that it appears he is dead. "Can you reach over and check to see if he is breathing?" She went on to suggest I place my hand on his chest or some other technique.

I approached the body, now within a foot and reached out with my hand to touch his exposed neck. I couldn't have been more shocked as this man's eyes slowly opened and looked curiously at me. This startled dude took a step back and told the operator "the man is alive."

I knelt beside this pathetic, emaciated young man and asked his name. He replied in a hoarse voice, "Chris." As the ambulance pulled up, Chris tried to raise his head, the flies swarming around us. I asked him just to relax. "I'm getting you some help."

Chris looked at me with a strange look and asked, "For what?"

I have seen and been through a lot, but that was a morning I won't ever forget. It's hard to put into words all my thoughts and emotions from that day. Mostly I just kept hearing those words "for what?" The disease of addiction is without limits a most ruinous disorder. My point for sharing that story is the one I have made in many classroom settings since. The formula for change is just that, not a formula for positive change necessarily but, just a formula for how we change.

I believe Chris at some point in his life, maybe when he was quite young, watched as someone popped open a beer and took a long drink. He watched them drink several more beers that day as they laughed with their friends and watched a game. When the men went outside to stretch their legs, Chris picked up the beer and smelled it. He probably looked around mischievously to make sure no one saw as he tasted for the first time the alcohol that would eventually lead to that ghastly morning when we met.

The thought of drinking planted like a seed, started to grow in Chris's mind. At what point Chris began drinking I don't know, but the thought blossomed into a behavior. What I do know is that when Chris took his first drink, he wasn't thinking to himself, "I can't wait to be a raging alcoholic." Never in a million years did he see himself laying in the weeds covered in flies.

How we as strugglers walk out of this almost certain destructive malady is the same way we got into it. The thoughts have to change, from arrogance to humility, from entitled to grateful. I know as you read these pages you are thinking, *There is no way I will end up like Chris.* That is probably the exact same thing Chris would have told me in his misguided self-confidence years earlier. I won't let this thing get out of control.

Change that leads to a life you can't imagine begins with your thoughts. It may be one in which, as an ex-convict, you see yourself years later working as facility coordinator for a men's residential rehab. You observe as men get their lives back on track, or wives and kids come back home and these young men changing the trajectory of their lives for generations to follow.

Or like the young boy tasting his first beer, he ignores the signs that his life is moving in a bad direction. Never changing his thoughts, this mother's son is found lying on the roadside ravaged by alcohol. Without that change in thinking, the kind that brings us to a place of humility and gratefulness, we are not willing or ready to be taught new behaviors. Can you see the correlation between the five steps up the ladder of recovery and the formula for change?

Thoughts → Humble, Grateful

Behavior → Teachable

Habits → Accountable

Character → Responsible

There it is, the formula for change — the kind of change that leads to recovery. For those of you who wish your struggling loved one was "more responsible," now you know why he or she isn't. Thoughts lead to behaviors that lead to habits that lead to character. Pride and rebellion never lead to character.

Trying to teach angry, entitled strugglers the values of maturity is a difficult, frustrating, and often fruitless endeavor. On the other hand, providing an opportunity for these addict/criminals to see the damage and hurt for which they have been responsible, helping them see how the trajectory of their life brought them to a place where their thoughts begin to change, providing an opportunity for someone to teach them new behaviors.

Direct, redirect, and self-direct — that is the teaching method. "Acting as if" is a principle widely used in rehabs nationwide. The idea is that we start practicing behaviors that may not be at all what we have been used to until they become new habits (acting like the person I want to become). We start with the most basic of behaviors. We wake up early, make our bed, clean our room, and get started on our life.

For some that is school or class, for others it is work. Regardless, it has routine, discipline, and purpose. The next principle is "social learning," learning what works and doesn't work by watching others' lives. The idea is that while some are moving ahead with their lives by practicing certain behaviors, others are holding on to pride and obstinance — and not progressing. The addict/criminal gets to choose what direction he or she would like to pursue based on the outcomes.

Please Don't Toss My Book

This will be the most difficult segment to write. I have had this conversation with many who have a loved one struggling as an addict/criminal. This is a place where I find it important to talk to these caregivers who have been abused, thus becoming strugglers themselves. I need to ask some difficult questions. I hope you will be open to what I am about to say.

I cannot begin to tell you the levels of abuse I have seen perpetrated on abused strugglers by other abused strugglers. I mean loved ones, family members, girlfriends, boyfriends, children, grandparents, and even great grandparents. I wrote this book for you as much as for the addict/criminal. In this world of addiction, all of us are strugglers.

I will not go into any detailed accounts because, quite honestly, they are sickening. As one who lived as an addict/criminal for many years, I must relive at times my abuse when I see similar abuses by others. *While I realize that addiction is the real culprit in many cases, this only explains the situation. It never excuses it!*

That being said, what is at times equally difficult to watch is the abused struggler accommodating the demands or "wants and needs" of their addict/criminal. It is not only pitiful to see how the addict/criminal has manipulated them through fear and intimidation, those who are willing to love them, willing to believe in them.

Watching interactions with these abused loved ones, as well as countless conversations I have had with those same abused love ones, leads me to a few recommendations. I hope you will consider my insight as you work through the very difficult task of getting help for your struggling addict/criminal.

I suspect your intentions are honest and stem from deep love and concern. When I was researching my last book, I read a story from a young man who had been watching a caterpillar go through its various stages. The day he saw the caterpillar, now presumably a butterfly, fighting and wiggling its way out of the cocoon, the young man attempted to help it by tearing open the cocoon.

The newly formed butterfly dropped from the cocoon and lay in the dirt until dead. Was the young man cruel? Hardly, for he was nurturing this process and held great hope for the process — but was improperly engaged. *He was quite simply uninformed of the value of the butterfly's need for struggle.*

An example of this is the parents who pay thousands of dollars for an attorney only to see this happen. Their struggler wants to be bailed out. The judge agrees to reduce the sentence for this addict/criminal if they go through rehab. These same parents pay again to make bail and put their struggler in rehab. On the day this addict/criminal is released to the rehab, the parents come to drop off some clothes only to be met with a list of "things I need," which they promptly go purchase.

A second motivation I witness is the "guilt factor." For months this addict/criminal has preached his abuse at these abused grandparents. He has guilted them with his life "where no one loved him, everyone abused him, how could they not understand" the addiction he had chosen.

The addict/criminal is not responsible for the thefts of money and property. After all, "you know I have a good heart." The grandparents or a single mother, who were not able to give this struggler "all they needed" growing up, in their guilt try to overcompensate by making this "poor struggler" more comfortable. They assume much of the guilt for allowing or causing this condition.

The last scenario I will propose is one in which co-dependency has produced an anomalous relationship. Mothers who have lost husbands turn to their sons to fill that void. A wife or girlfriend so insecure and terrified of being "alone" will choose the dysfunction of an abusive struggler and will even choose at times to go without or neglect the needs of a child to cater to this entitled and abusive addict/criminal. Men who compromise everything for the affection or attention of an abusive addict/criminal only to watch her trade sex for her addiction again and again.

Let me emphasize clearly the role you can play in helping the addict/criminal reach that place of humility and gratefulness — and it is for you to do less, not more. People invest in what they value, so you must expect your struggler to invest. Expect the struggler to invest now, not a promise to do so in the future. Expect the struggler to complete the first phase of rehab or attend outpatient counseling without begging, guilting, or quitting.

When they don't follow through, make sure there is a penalty. We wouldn't pay the lawn kid if he didn't finish the job or never showed up, but your daughter gets a pass when she reneges on a promise or commitment. Make them invest, help create humility. Going without can create gratitude. When you give in, it creates an attitude of entitlement.

Let them sit, let them stress, let them go without, let them struggle. Do you know what they will be thinking about?

Their choices, their recklessness. They will wrestle with guilt, they will imagine a life without you, and those are good things. Eventually, you will reach a breaking point. Enough will be enough. Why not now? Are you ready to see the process of change begin?

If what I have written has either touched something inside you or has generated a 50-pound wrecking ball response in your mind, consider that what I am sharing may be based on an element of truth. Seek help, seek advice, use the references in the back of the book before you take another step with your loved one. In your efforts to help, what if you are tearing open the cocoon?

A Few Coins For Your Change Jar:

- Are you, like many, trying to affect change by starting with habits?

- What influences are steering your thoughts? Do you understand "acting as if"? How are you putting that into practice?

- Have a conversation with young Chris about that beer he just tasted.

CHAPTER 27

A Chapter To My
Christian Friends

I have been asked some interesting questions over the years about recovery and Christianity. As a rule, these questions seem to imply some perceived contradiction between the two. One question will be along the lines of "Why do I need the Big Book when I have the Bible?" The question seems to imply that the two books represent two theologies and that by choosing one you must deny the other. I understand the question but see it as comparing apples with oranges.

The Bible is inspired by God and made up of 66 books written by more than 40 authors over a 1,500-year period. The Big Book was written by Bill W. and Dr. Bob and it took them five years. The Big Book has some valuable information that has helped a large multitude of addicts find their way out of alcoholism. The Big Book draws from a spirituality that has its roots in the Bible, not the other way around. That said, all truth has its roots in God, and we should never fear truth no matter where it is found. Additionally, many Christian authors have written extensively on addiction and have drawn from or referenced aspects of the Big Book.

I attended a meeting once where the speaker talked about his life being unmanageable and in his despair, he cried out to God as he understood him. I felt touched in my heart that night and cried out to God as I understood him. My experience happened in a church meeting referred to as a revival. Quite naturally I and everyone who ever lived and cried out to God has done so "as they understood him."

Anyone who says they fully understand God and therefore everyone else is wrong, is a person I suggest you avoid. The question about "God as I understand him" becoming a major hangup for Christians is justified. The recovery community has at times made this a tenet of their "faith" and ostracized those who articulate Jesus as the God of their understanding.

Recovery is a personal, spiritual journey that one shares with God and family (community). Jesus and I have been on this journey together since 1989. I hurt for those who oppose His place in creation and His sovereignty in the recovery process. At the same time, I marvel at His unlimited grace and aspire to reflect some version of that light and grace.

Rejecting out of hand the need to attend meetings based on a bias about this issue of "who God is" would be first contrary to Scripture that charges "we are light and salt" to the world. We can bring a new perspective (light) without being offensive. For those who feel that AA or NA meetings "leave a bad taste in your mouth," add some salt.

Will NA or AA lead my struggling loved one away from God? It can if that is their only spiritual diet. The twelfth step says, "having had a spiritual awakening as a result of these steps ..." Even the writers saw the steps as pointing us away from "self" (the god of my understanding as an addict/criminal) and towards God (Almighty Creator) — away from selfishness and toward service to others.

Relationship and balance become an issue. Is it biblical principles or the Twelve Steps? The answer is both — in balanced portions. The study and reading of the Bible should be a lifelong, every day kind of habit. The Twelve Steps, while valuable, should not in any way be "canonized" and find equal footing with Scripture — nor can they become a basis for genuine faith.

I believe that Celebrate Recovery style meetings are a great balance, giving God's word a preeminent place in recovery. CR also recognizes Jesus as our "higher power." CR will always emphasize a relationship with Jesus which is the "edge" Christians have in recovery.

The fact is that the addict/criminal has a worship problem. No, I'm not talking about the singing that churches do before the preacher gets up to speak. Worship is the honor, adoration, and sacrifice given to a supreme being or deity. We are by nature (our creative purpose) creatures who worship. Therefore, it is not whether we will choose to worship, but rather who or what we will worship.

The Bible begins with God as the Creator who is worthy of our awe and worship. He is a provider, healer, teacher, savior, and when we see Him clearly, we worship Him. As an addict/criminal, we attempt to fill the role of all the aforementioned with self-worship. It's all about our efforts, our pleasure, and our comfort. We "create worlds" but find ourselves powerless to put out the fires when they start burning.

When I cried out to God about an addiction I couldn't stop, I heard something in my spirit say, "You get out of that habit the same way you got in it: Worship!" I love how the NIV Bible translates Hebrews 12:2: "Fix your eyes on Jesus." Turns out I needed a different fix. Sadly, no one will find worship disorder listed in their diagnosis or treatment plan. (I digress.)

I cannot end this segment without addressing medications and what if any role they should play in the recovery of a Christian. Mental health medications, like medications for specific physical ailments, are subject to the source of the diagnosis and the competence and compassion of the source of the treatment plan. Does not God heal all such ailments if one has enough faith? No, He does not. Yes, He can with a breath raise the dead! He can heal the most helpless of conditions, yet that is not always the case, and we cannot demand that He do so or conjure up healing with some "mystical level" of faith.

To the point, seek the counsel of others, do your homework, and proceed slowly and with caution when it comes to medications in general — but specifically with mental health meds. My experience with certain clients is that medication given correctly and in the correct dosage can produce remarkable results.

I am aware as well that medications can be abused, misdiagnosed, and actually exacerbate a mental health issue if not closely monitored and used in moderation. Medication can be particularly useful in a mental health crisis to avoid injury to the struggler or healthcare professionals. Do not dismiss the idea wholesale because of some religious notion that Jesus doesn't like medication.

Advances in surgery, therapeutic medications, and cures for diseases are, at their core, God's creative character maximized in mankind. Ideally, medications would not be an element of one's physical or mental health regimen. However, practically I do not see that as a reality for all people at all times.

In my book *Monsters and Butterflies*, I speak directly to transformation as the ideal process of recovery. I will work and pray to the end that everyone in my realm of influence experience a transformational relationship with Jesus. My bottom line, I suppose, is that we do not use Christianity as a reason not to attend meetings, nor should we use Christianity as a reason to forgo rehab. We also do not condemn the twelve steps as somehow anti-biblical. We do not speak of those who are reliant upon the twelve steps as ignorant or weak, for Jesus does not condone or validate that position.

Use your heads as you live and work among outsiders. Don't miss a trick. Make the most of every opportunity. Be gracious in your speech. The goal is to bring out the best in others in a conversation, not put them down, not cut them out. (Colossians 4:6 MSG)

I have watched men flourish in rehabs that were not "faith-based," watched men grow from truths espoused by those who do not champion Christianity. I have watched men grow into men of God with character, even while attending NA meetings that don't really "do the Jesus thing." The God I serve and worship is so much bigger than our opinions. His grace is beyond our understanding.

I sat on our screened-in back porch looking out over the lake, the water like a mirror. The sun was setting and the color was filling the reflection. My wife came out and sat next to me, and we talked about the eagle perched on the dock. For just a moment, I remembered walking around the inside perimeter fence of Tomoka State Prison telling God how nice it would be just to sit by a river with a beautiful wife with no screaming and yelling, no TV blasting — just quiet.

There I was years later living my dream. I never actually prayed that as a prayer. It was just God and I talking. As a Christian, I have been blessed beyond description. Our lives have not been without struggle. We have had tragedy and pain. Jesus walked with us through it all. We have Jesus, we have each other, we have community. We live on purpose.

CHAPTER 28

A Chapter To My Skeptical Friends

"In the beginning, God created." Can you think of a more controversial statement? While millions would agree with that statement, millions more would ardently disagree. You have to love the fact that the number one best-selling book of all time in human history begins with those words.

Please allow me to make a similar statement that is far less controversial, one I would like to discuss briefly as it relates to recovery. "In the beginning was relationships." Perhaps we can agree that statement must be true. Three things necessary for anything similar to our earth or the life that exists here are:

Matter → proton – neutron – electron (the atom). The building blocks.

Space → length – width – height (space). A place to build.

Time → past – present – future (a marked event. Building begins.

Matter moving through space at a specific time produced everything we understand. Creation or Big

Bang can be argued, but not relationships, the common denominator that is perhaps the essential element of this equation. Relationships are the activity of development. The "higher power," he, she, they, or it operates in the harmony of relationships.

I have long argued with those who are concerned about issues related to addiction that we cannot overemphasize the importance of community in the recovery process. Recovery is a personal process that must be shared with a "higher power" and other people. The addict/criminal is a selfish loner even in a crowded room. They live in a world of transactions, all the while aching for relationships. It is not sustainable to live apart from relationships, nothing works or certainly doesn't work well.

Regardless of your position or worldview, if I may be so bold, you as an addict/criminal are not the "higher power." You are not strong enough or smart enough, and you do not possess enough resources to keep your world in orbit without relationships. I know you say, "Jim, I don't do church and Jesus," and I get it. I don't do aliens and apes but we have this in common — we all need relationships. The life you are looking for, the reason you are pain killing, is that your life is not connected. ... Relationship is the issue.

The Counselor Kid

I never in a million years saw myself going to a therapist. I would have laughed in your face had you suggested such. That of course was before I got serious about recovery. If the first step of recovery is being truly sick of living in a way that always ends up hurting others, I was there.

After spending 13 years in prison, I was out, but still struggling with addict/criminal behavior. I was not using, I was not committing crimes, but I was deceptive, keeping secrets, and manipulating people for personal benefit. I was in danger of losing everything and everybody, and I knew the signs.

When someone suggested I go see "Neil," I thought, *What do I have to lose?* I walked into the office and saw a 25-year-old kid right out of school sitting in front of me. Immediately I thought, *Ok, I've already spent the money, but this is a one-and-done moment.* Turns out this kid was pretty smart, came off as real, and certainly acted older than he looked. We talked and I walked away with a different attitude. Long story short: This went on for a few months, and we began talking about some pretty tough stuff.

There was one morning in particular that was a life-changer. I came in as usual and we engaged in a little small talk. Then Neil said something like, "I want to talk to you about intimacy." In a nano-second, I felt the blood rise in my neck. I am sure my arms folded across my chest as I sat back in my seat with a sneering smile.

If this kid thinks I am going to discuss my sex life with him, he's fixing to get the surprise of his little life. What the heck is wrong with this dude? I was ready to pounce! He looked at me and said, "Does that bother you? "I lied and said, "Maybe a little."

Neil looked at me and with words I will never forget said, "It bothers you because you don't even know what that word means. You think I wanted to talk about sexuality. Can I tell you what that word means?"

Intimacy is being fully known and fully loved. He went on to tell me intimacy is what I have been looking for all my life, a relationship in which I could be fully honest without fear of rejection — a relationship that didn't require performance, but was mask free, face to face.

He was right. All my relationships were guarded, portrayals of who I wanted people to think I was. They were built on the underlying motive, "What do I have to give to get what I want?" Not having that relationship was the source of a lot of unresolved pain that I tried to numb with drugs, sex, anger. Not having that relationship threw my life out of orbit.

"Remember we deal with addiction: cunning,
baffling, powerful! Without help (relationship) it is
too much for us. But there is One who has all power
— that One is God. May you find Him now."
Paraphrased excerpt from How It Works

Epilogue

Doing nothing is not an option. Once we accept that, we realize that every situation is unique and has variables. I hope you have a perspective you didn't necessarily have before reading this book. I pray my words will be valuable as you choose what happens next. Seek help and do it today, it doesn't get better with time. At the very least, decide that you are unable to decide and find those who can help you move in a positive direction. Please don't fall prey to the deception of false contentment that comes, for some, when they realize they have heard the truth. Hearing is not enough unless it leads to doing.

If you are currently using or you are a caregiver of someone who is, the first step is detox. This process ranges from a few days to a few weeks. The type and severity of drug usage determine that. If your loved one is struggling with the addict/criminal lifestyle, you have choices. For many, we find ourselves "backed into a corner," sometimes of our own doing. We have convinced ourselves that everyone has given up on the situation and we are left alone to carry the weight of the burden. There are hundreds of people who can and will help.

For some, we try to keep the "secret" of our addiction or that of the struggler living in our home. If we slipped and fell at home, our ankle blue and swollen, the pain too much to allow us to walk properly, we would go to a clinic and seek treatment immediately. Smoking meth, shooting heroin, or drinking until drunk every day are far more deadly and also require action.

It is pride that keeps us from seeking help. I remember getting a call late one evening from a young lady who told us her boyfriend was outside screaming filthy words and threatening her. When I asked the young lady if she had called law enforcement or a crisis intervention unit, she replied, "No, I don't want to get him in trouble."

This response is not unusual. After many conversations over the years with parents and loved ones of the addict/criminal, I get it. The idea that intervention when the struggler is in crisis or has crossed certain boundaries regarding their safety or the safety of others is a tough one.

Your struggler is already in trouble. That is exactly what I told the young lady that night: "Do you want to save his life? Do you want to see the struggler escape this insidious lifestyle that has stolen who he is?" I ask you the same questions. Are you prepared to make the tough decisions that the addict/criminal is incapable of making? Love is risky business. It is not contingent on a reciprocal response; it just loves.

The reason your struggler continues to use is that they are able to do so. Drugs and alcohol cost money. Addict/criminals find that money, a place to sleep, and some food. Never should they get those from anyone unconditionally if you know about their addiction. Please, before you say that I have not had to deal with this at a personal level, I assure you I have. I know it is a crushing weight.

I will work for any addict/criminal willing to work with me, but that is not negotiable. I will take a step and maybe two, but they will know in advance what steps I expect from them. I have been doing this long enough to know that I can't help everyone I want to help. Everyone who needs help doesn't want it. They want you to understand that and they want you to pay for them to continue to live as they please. Their words will say otherwise, but their actions will demonstrate rejection of meaningful conversations about change.

Ask yourself this question: "If what is going on in my house was being done by someone I didn't know, would I allow it?" Listen to the excuses flying through your mind! I then challenge you to call an attorney's office and tell them, "I let a stranger move in and now they are drunk all night and sleeping all day. They are stealing and threatening and cursing. What should I do?" Be willing to listen to their dumbfounded response.

My intention for writing this book is first and foremost to bring light to the struggle that has reached epidemic proportions in our country. I hope to inform and then challenge the assumptions of the addict/criminal mindset. I pray you will now be better prepared to have a meaningful conversation with your loved one. I pray you will be able to take this information and develop a game plan for how to rescue the struggler.

And if you are the addict/criminal struggler, I hope you find the grace and courage to recognize that the actions of your loved ones, while seemingly punitive and uncaring, are actually the opposite. If you are caught in the grip of addiction, I pray you will rise to a new perspective, surrender, and ask God and those like me for help. We have chosen to fight the fight against this enemy and walk with you.

Let me end by offering you the two most life-changing words ever spoken. They are certainly far more than just words, for they carry the power of transformation when fully realized by any human anywhere. These words transcend time, culture, demographics, and language. These terms are not separate and apart from the subject of this book. Know that these words permeate each page as I wrote out the chapters. I like to think of these words as two sides of the same coin.

My life story explains me, it does not excuse me. On the other hand, these two words define me. They are the reason I am married today, the reason I am not languishing in some prison, bitter and alone. They are the reason I am alive, the reason I have enjoyed a life filled with unspeakable joy and survived unbearable pain.

Whatever situation confronts me must pass through the prism of these two words. They are a fortification that surrounds me. They are a drive inside me. I have never seen a life that cannot be radically changed when these words are added to the equation. These words are the only words I can speak about as an expert, having done a life study of 60 years. Yet my ability to harness them with language still eludes me.

It is the answer to mankind's hostility. Everyone who claims freedom did so and will do so by walking down the path carved out by these words. When you hear the cry of a newborn child, it is a testament to these words. When you see a family holding hands and singing at the grave of a loved one, it is a chorus sung in honor of these words. The atheist who sits on the beach contemplating the beauty of the natural order of the world and inhales a breath in preparation of exhaling words of dispute towards the God of creation does so only under the power and authority of these two words: *grace* and *mercy*.

Grace is quite simply undeserved favor. God gifted me with something I do not deserve. He has done so in ways that, like Isaiah the prophet, I want to fall on the ground and hide my face for I am a man of unclean lips. Yet, grace has nothing to do with me and everything to do with the greatness of God. I accept His grace as an act of worship. I am on display in this world as one who in my brokenness is chosen to represent God in His message of grace.

Grace has infused the lens of my worldview. It is the ink spilled across the pages of my indictment. I live and love and work and die a little more each day with one over-arching goal, and that is to hear God say to me "Well done." The boldness of such an expectation is in and through His grace as well.

Mercy is the other side of the coin and it represents undeserved pardon. It is God withholding that which I deserved. My life as an addict/criminal was reckless. For every brush with death I experienced, I am certain there were dozens more that went unnoticed — the cars I never collided with, the guns that did not fire or missed their mark, the diagnosis I never got, the tragedies that were somehow averted.

Grace and mercy are messy concepts. No measure of "fairness" can be applied to them, which is why we grapple with their ramifications. In truth, the only qualification one needs to receive them is to be undeserving.

I was part of perhaps the most unique "Bible study" on grace and mercy ever, and it began on the side of a road.

Guardian of the Homeless

Some years back, I was returning from what had become a weekly visit to a prison in central Florida. The hour-long ride led through an undeveloped stretch of highway with no businesses for miles. One afternoon I saw what appeared to be a man walking his bike in the middle of nowhere, stranded no doubt, as the afternoon sun was dropping. I pulled my truck to the side of the road and waited as he came alongside me. This unkempt young man was about 30 and I surmised he was a drifter. Then I noticed his bike, loaded with what few personal belongings he possessed, had no tires, only rims.

I told the young man I was going to a town about 30 miles away and I could give him a ride if he wanted to put his bike in the back. That's when I noticed the machete protruding from the backpack he was wearing. I suggested at this point that maybe he could put the backpack with the bike, which he did, and I resumed breathing.

We sat in the front seat looking at each other for a few seconds. He thought I was a cop and I thought he was a serial killer. The ride was interesting, to say the least. I asked how he got so far from anywhere and he was only too glad to tell me. Turned out this young man was in his own words the "guardian of the homeless," a warrior defending the weak and vulnerable from "the enemy." He looked at me very intensely when he asked, "You know who the enemy is, right?" I was sure I did, but wondered what might be his answer, so I had to ask, and he told me: "female doctors."

I don't know if you have ever been in the proximity of a homeless drifter who smelled like smoke and dirty socks, who had in his possession a machete, with no one around for miles, who just revealed an extreme level of delusional thinking. It will cause one to question every decision one has ever made, especially about picking up strangers.

My self-preservation mode kicked in and I said to him, "I believe Jesus can overcome any enemy." Just like that, the conversation took a turn. He questioned the validity of Scripture, the basic premise of the gospel, and he took particular exception to the idea "that any father would let his son die for something he didn't do, especially for crimes he knew that others committed." This was not incoherent rambling. This guy had thought through the issues to some degree.

The answer I gave him spoke of a love only God possessed and how trying to understand God from a human perspective would always fall short. We engaged in more back-and-forth conversation and before we knew it, we were in a town where he felt good about being dropped off. Death having been averted once again, I then felt safe to return to my life. I would chalk this experience up to zeal and put it to rest. However, the conversation felt incomplete, and my answers seemed pat. When I got home, I began searching the Scriptures to pursue an answer I should have given to his question: "Why would a father force or even ask his son or anyone he loved to die for the crimes of another?"

When I came upon the answer, it brought me freedom I was not expecting. The answer is found in 2nd

Corinthians: *"For He made Him who knew no sin to be sin for us, that we might become the righteousness of God in Him"* (2 Corinthians 5:21, emphasis added). Martin Luther referred to this as "the great exchange." God *became* sin so that we could *become* righteous. Neither seems possible (or fair), yet it was the only answer to a fallen world. He died for the sin He became. I stand righteous in the presence of indescribable holiness because I became righteous. He took on my nature and I was given His. He could not have sinned; I am incapable of righteousness apart from this cataclysmic event best characterized as grace and mercy. That grace and mercy are available to you, whoever you are, wherever you are. He is one prayer away; may you find Him now in your hour of greatest need.

Jim Adkins

Resources

National Suicide Prevention Lifeline — 800-273-8255

National Helpline — 800-662-HELP (4357) www.samhsa.gov
Treatment referral and information, 24/7.

American Association of Christian Counselors —
www.aacc.net

Partnership to End Addiction — drugfree.org

Mayo Clinic — mayoclinic.org/intervention

Celebrate Recovery — celebraterecovery.com

National Parent Hotline —nationalparenthelpline.org

Liberty Ranch Rehab Center —thelibertyranch.com
comprehensive resource page

Mental health Gateway —mentalhealthgateway.org

American Residential Treatment Association —artausa.org

Narcotics Anonymous — na.org

Continued →

Must-Read Books

Crash the Chatterbox, Steven Furtick

Don't Call it Love, Dr. Tim Clinton

Man in the Mirror, Patrick Morely

Manhood Restored, Eric Mason

Monsters and Butterflies; Making Sense of Change, Jim Adkins

Redeeming Love, Francine Rivers

The Two-Minute Drill to Manhood, John Croyle

Wild at Heart, John Eldridge

You're Not Crazy — You're Codependent, Jeanette Elisabeth Menter

Must-See Videos

A Beautiful Design (Matt Chandler)

Authentic Manhood

Celebrate Recovery Official

Chasing the Dragon; The Life of an Opiate Addict

Lecrae's Story

Sobrietytelevision

Stand 4 Recovery

Unmasked: The Stigma of Meth

Made in the USA
Middletown, DE
03 September 2024